The Allocation of Corporate Indirect Costs

James M. Fremgen
and
Shu S. Liao
Naval Postgraduate School

National Association of Accountants
Montvale, N.J.

Published by
National Association of Accountants
10 Paragon Drive, P.O. Box 433, Montvale, N.J. 07645-0433

NAA Publication Number 81130
ISBN 0-86641-006-6

Foreword

The allocation of indirect costs is one of the most common and yet one of the most controversial practices in accounting. In general, theorists say it cannot be done; still, practitioners do it. This research study seeks to determine the extent to which business firms do allocate corporate indirect costs among their primary profit centers, how they do it, and why they do it. The observations of actual practice are correlated with the familiar theoretical arguments to provide a basis for understanding and evaluating both. Data on actual practices were obtained from a survey of 123 corporations in various industries and various size groups. Comparisons of practices among the firms in the different categories are provided here.

Indirect cost allocations are frequently considered in the context of external financing reporting. This study, however, focuses on the uses of allocations for management accounting purposes. Specifically, both theoretical analysis and practical applications were studied in relation to three important management objectives: internal performance evaluation, cost-based pricing, and decision analysis. The findings of this study document the widespread use of allocations for these purposes and help to explain why they are used in spite of the overwhelming theoretical injunctions against them.

Guidance in the development of the research questionnaire and the final research report was provided by the Project Committee:

Henry M. Klein
General Instrument Corporation
El Paso, Texas

Robert W. Liptak
Bigelow-Sanford, Inc.
Greenville, South Carolina

Carl M. Koontz
ALCOA
Alcoa, Tennessee

Ronald J. Patten
University of Connecticut
Storrs, Connecticut

This report reflects the views of the authors, and not necessarily those of the National Association of Accountants, its Committee on Research, or the Project Committee.

Stephen Landekich
Research Director
National Association of Accountants

Table of Contents

List of Tables

Chapter 1

Introduction

Cost allocation has been featured prominently in the accounting literature and practiced for many years. At the outset, it is necessary to recognize that there are two quite different notions of cost allocation. The first is the allocation of costs among time periods. Examples of such allocations are depreciation or amortization of long-lived assets and various inventory costing methods, such as FIFO and LIFO. Indeed, such intertemporal cost allocations play a major role in the accrual basis of accounting. Thus, it is not surprising that allocations over time have been the subject of most discussions of cost allocation in financial accounting.

The second notion of allocation is the allocation of costs among cost objectives within a period. Examples include allocations of manufacturing overhead costs to products, allocations of service center costs among production departments, and allocations of general and administrative expenses among the segments of a firm. This second notion of cost allocation has been dominant in the literature of cost accounting and managerial accounting. This study focuses only on allocations of costs among cost objectives. Allocations over time will be given only brief attention.

Nature of Indirect Cost Allocation

The allocation of indirect costs among cost objectives is closely associated with the divisionalization of business operations. The rationale for divisionalized operations lies in the presumed behavioral advantages of operating quasi-autonomous profit centers in a decentralized organization so that the creative talents of segment managers will be encouraged to develop in a climate of delegated authority. In this situation, any costs assigned to a profit center from some other source become important elements in that profit center's performance. If such cost assignments are determined arbitrarily, they may distort reported performance and lead to inappropriate evaluations of profit center managers.

Two parallel but conceptually distinct problems accompany the assignment of costs to a profit center from some other source. The first is the determination of appropriate transfer prices for goods or services transferred between profit centers. The second is the allocation of indirect costs incurred by the company to those segments presumed to benefit from those indirect costs. The indirect cost allocation problem is more pervasive than transfer pricing because it arises in every organization that recognizes distinct segments and may exist at various levels in the organization.

Issues in Indirect Cost Allocation

A profit center is a part of the total organization and, therefore, is presumed to benefit to some extent from the indirect, or common, costs incurred by the organization. The problem is to determine the appropriate amount of indirect cost to be charged to each profit center. There is general agreement in the accounting literature that indirect cost allocations are inevitably arbitrary. It is argued that they may be intuitively appealing and seemingly precise but are still arbitrary because they seek to divide something that is inherently indivisible. Thus, indirect cost allocations are made in practice only because management perceives a need for them. If this need is not made very specific, however, there is no basis for determining whether current indirect cost allocation practices are really appropriate.

Three important questions need to be answered with respect to indirect cost allocations:

1. Can allocations ever be made reliably?
2. For what purposes should cost allocations be or not be made?
3. On what bases should indirect costs be allocated?

Obviously, the first question is logically prior to the next two. If there were general agreement on a negative answer to this question, it would be pointless to pursue the other two. Issues related to these three questions will be discussed briefly here. An extensive review of the literature on these issues will be found in Chapter 2.

Can Allocations Ever Be Made Reliably?

Unquestionably, it is possible, mechanically, to allocate indirect costs among cost objectives. Accountants have been doing it for many years. One may question, however, whether it is possible to make allocations in such a way that the resultant costs meet reasonable criteria for accounting information. Relevance and reliability have been suggested as the two primary qualities of accounting information.[1] Thus, cost allocations should be both relevant to the intended purposes of the users of the resulting information and reliable in the sense that those users may trust the allocations to measure what they purport to measure. Reliability includes such characteristics as objectivity, freedom from bias, neutrality, and verifiability.[2] If one accepts relevance and reliability as valid criteria for accounting information, the acceptability of indirect cost allocations has to depend upon their meeting those criteria.

Why Should Indirect Cost Allocations Be or Not Be Made?

As mentioned earlier, indirect cost allocations are made only because management perceives a need for them. The nature of this need has not really been made specific, however. Thus, one may reasonably ask, "For what purposes are indirect cost allocations needed or useful?" Most discussions of the objectives of indirect cost allocations have addressed one or more of the following four distinct areas:

1. Financial reporting, in which cost allocations are used to value assets and to determine segment income.
2. Planning and decision analysis, in which cost allocations are used to predict the financial effects of future actions.
3. Pricing, in which cost allocations are used to establish appropriate selling prices.
4. Performance evaluation and control, in which cost allocations are used to influence managers' behavior with respect to costs.

These four areas are consistent with those cited in widely used cost accounting texts, although the wordings are not identical.[3] Distinctions among the four categories may not be absolutely clear in all cases. Planning and control are obviously related activities, and pricing is, of course, a specific instance of decision making. Nevertheless, they will help to focus the discussion in Chapter 2 of the broad and diverse literature on indirect cost allocation.

How Should Indirect Cost Allocations Be Made?

The methodology of indirect cost allocations involves two principal issues: What separate pools of indirect costs should be identified and allocated together? Over what base should the costs in any given pool be allocated? Both of these issues, but particularly the latter, depend upon the objective of the allocation. For example, if the allocation is made to satisfy some broadly worded requirement, management is likely to establish only a few broad indirect cost pools and to allocate them over some readily available bases. Ease and convenience are the dominant considerations. If the requirement is not specific and if management has little interest in the allocations, it is only natural that the easiest acceptable methods will be chosen. On the other hand, if management wishes to allocate costs in order to induce a particular response on the part of division managers, there are likely to be more indirect cost pools and more carefully selected allocation bases.

The issues of the composition of an indirect cost pool and the allocation base are not unrelated, of course. Chapter 2 considers how the selection of an allocation base affects the composition of a cost pool, what the criteria are for choosing an allocation base, and how the selection of the base is affected by the objective of the cost allocation. Methods of indirect cost allocation actually used by business firms are reported in Chapter 4.

Objective and Scope of the Study

Objective

The basic objective of this study is to determine current business practices with respect to the allocation of indirect costs for various purposes and the reasons for these practices. Indirect cost allocations have been discussed extensively in the accounting literature. However, very few writers have looked explicitly into current cost allocation practices and the rationale behind them. This study will investigate how various indirect costs commonly incurred by business corporations are classified, to what extent these costs are allocated, on what bases they are allocated, and for what reasons allocations are considered appropriate and inappropriate. A critique of current practices and several recommendations then will be made.

Scope

This study focuses specifically on the practices currently being used to allocate the indirect costs incurred by a corporation among its primary profit centers. The principal reason for focusing on the primary, or highest, level of segment responsibility rather than at lower levels in the organization is that allocations from corporate headquarters to primary profit centers are generally the same over all such centers. Allocation practices at lower levels of responsibility, on the other hand, may differ from segment to segment within a firm.

Definition of Terms

A lack of universal acceptance is characteristic of accounting terminology, especially of terms used in management accounting. Some terms have been used variously with different meanings. Furthermore, different terms have often been used to denote a single concept. At the practical level, terms usually have specific and well-understood meanings within individual companies. Unfortunately, their usage is not uniform among companies. To avoid possible confusion, certain terms used in this study are defined at the outset.

Indirect Costs

This term refers to costs incurred for the benefit of two or more components of a company in such a way that it is difficult or impossible to trace specific portions of the costs exclusively to individual components. Indirect costs are synonymous with "common costs" but are in direct contrast to "direct costs," which are wholly and exclusively traceable to a single component.

Primary Profit Center

This broadly inclusive term denotes the principal components of a company for which separate financial performances are reported. They may be described specifically as subsidiaries, business units, groups, divisions, departments, branches, or product lines. In companies that have a hierarchy of components at various levels of management responsibility, the primary profit centers are those at the highest level of separate responsibility. At various points in this study, the terms "division" and "segment" are used as synonyms for "primary profit center," simply for variety in the text.

Performance Evaluation

This is the periodic internal measurement and reporting of the financial performance of a primary profit center. Typically, actual performance is compared with predetermined performance criteria, such as target profit or return on investment.

Cost-Based Pricing

This term refers to any policy under which prices of products or services are based either wholly or substantially on the individual seller's costs. It is in contrast to the situation in which prices are determined entirely by competitive market forces.

Decision Analysis

This term is used to denote management's analysis of the expected financial consequences of a proposed decision involving a choice among alternatives. Examples of such decisions include the introduction of new products, the choice of optimal product mixes, the making or buying of parts, and the replacement of equipment.

Financial Reporting

This is the periodic preparation of financial statements in accordance with the requirements of the Financial Accounting Standards Board or of some regulatory agency, principally for use by parties external to the reporting organization.

Methodology of the Study

This study consists of four successive phases, including both library and empirical investigations.

1. *Library Research.* The conceptual foundation for the empirical work done in this study is an extensive review of the pertinent literature. The library research was conducted first in order to set current practices in a context of issues widely discussed in the literature. A questionnaire was then designed to provide empirical evidence relating to these issues.

2. *Questionnaire Survey.* The questionnaire was mailed to 766 companies, selected from the 1979 edition of *Standard & Poor's Register of Corporations* according to the following two criteria: (1) Annual sales were at least $15 million and (2) at least two executives were designated as being responsible for separate operating divisions, groups, departments, and so on. The questionnaire was accompanied by a cover letter signed by the research director of the National Association of Accountants and by a brief explanation of the scope of the questionnaire and the terms used in it. (The complete questionnaire appears in Appendix B.)

3. *In-Depth Personal Interviews.* On the basis of a preliminary analysis of the questionnaires returned, a set of questions was prepared for in-depth interviews, which were conducted with executives at nine firms on the West Coast. The objective of these interviews was to explore the rationale behind certain practices and to explore some issues raised by respondents to the questionnaire.

4. *Analysis and Evaluation of Practices.* A statistical analysis of responses to the questionnaire, along with the results of the literature review, formed the basis for an evaluation of current indirect cost allocation practices.

A more detailed discussion of the research procedures employed in this study is presented in Appendix A.

Summary of Findings and Conclusions

Despite the overwhelming objections to indirect cost allocations found in the literature, most companies responding to the survey reported allocating corporate indirect costs among their primary profit centers. One reason for this widespread practice of cost allocation can be seen in an analysis of the nature of indirect costs.

Distinguishing between direct and indirect costs is not as clear-cut as the accounting literature implies. Theoretically, traceability is the general criterion for classifying costs as direct. In practice, other factors also play significant roles in the classification of costs as direct or indirect. This fact suggests that traceability is either inadequate as a criterion or is subject to different managerial interpretations. Other factors affecting the classification of costs as direct or indirect include where the costs are incurred, why they are incurred, the size of the firm, the firm's management philosophy with respect to centralization or decentralization, and, to a lesser extent, the industry in which the firm operates.

The diversity of factors affecting the classification of indirect costs may help to explain the varying amounts of corporate costs reported by respondents as indirect. Corporate indirect costs ranged from as low as 0.02% to as high as 44% of revenue and were fairly evenly distributed between these extremes. With one exception, firms in different industries did not have significantly different percentages of indirect costs. The one exception was in banking, where banks consistently reported substantially larger proportions of indirect costs.

Respondents clearly distinguished between two types of corporate indirect costs: corporate administrative costs and corporate service costs. This distinction is particularly significant in that a much stronger case can be made for allocating corporate service costs than for allocating corporate administrative costs.

Causal and beneficial factors were most frequently cited as the criteria for choosing allocation bases, yet the bases actually used to allocate indirect costs do not reflect these criteria. Most respondents reported using allocation bases that, in effect, reflect an ability-to-bear criterion. A substantial number of respondents, however, did use bases reflecting causal factors to allocate corporate service costs.

According to respondents, the single most important reason for allocating indirect costs for performance evaluation is to remind profit center managers that indirect costs exist and that profit center earnings must be adequate to cover some share of those costs. The popularity of this reason may explain why indirect costs are allocated more often for performance evaluation than for the other three purposes addressed in the survey. This reason is essentially behavioral in nature. It implies that a precise determination of the "correct" cost may not be the intent of indirect cost allocation. Instead, the allocation is intended to condition the behavior of profit center managers in some positive way.

An important behavioral requirement for cost allocations is that they not violate the principle of cost controllability. Since profit center managers can control their usage of corporate services, allocating corporate service costs is both defensible and potentially desirable. Such allocations should be at predetermined rates rather than actual rates, however, so that unplanned efficiency or inefficiency on the part of corporate staffs is not passed on to the profit centers. Profit center managers, of course, cannot control efficiency in the corporate staffs. In practice, though, more respondents use actual amounts of indirect costs in allocations than use predetermined amounts.

In order for indirect cost allocations to reflect the extent of profit centers' use of corporate services, it is necessary to distinguish between variable and fixed costs and to allocate them separately. Variable indirect costs should be allocated at predetermined rates on the basis of actual usage, whereas fixed indirect costs should be allocated in a single predetermined lump sum. In practice, however, relatively few companies do allocate fixed and variable costs separately.

The dominant reasons given by survey respondents for allocating indirect costs for purposes of cost-based pricing were all variations of a single theme—the desire to recover a fair share of all costs through the prices of all product lines. What constitutes a "fair" share is, of course, inherently subjective. Thus, the objective here again appears to be primarily behavioral in nature.

Indirect cost allocations are even less appropriate for decision analysis than for the other purposes. Indirect cost allocations *per se* should not be included in decision analyses. It is possible, however, that current allocation rates may be acceptable surrogates for the true but unknown amounts of incremental indirect costs.

The widespread use of ability-to-bear allocation bases, such as gross sales or total assets, actually may be compatible with the motivational objectives of indirect cost allocations that were reported by a majority of the respondents. If indirect cost allocations are made primarily for behavioral reasons, broad measures of activity or size are less objectionable than theory would suggest; in this case, the mere fact of the allocations is more important than the amounts. On the other hand, if the purpose is to measure cost or profit figures that will be regarded as "correct," allocations should be limited to variable corporate service costs and allocation bases should represent true causal factors.

Notes

1. *Qualitative Characteristics of Accounting Information*, Statement of Financial Accounting Concepts No. 2 (Stamford, Conn.: Financial Accounting Standards Board, 1980), pages 14–15.

2. *Ibid.*

3. Charles T. Horngren, *Cost Accounting: A Managerial Emphasis*, 4th edition (Englewood Cliffs, N.J.: Prentice-Hall, Inc., 1977), pages 501–502; and Gordon Shillinglaw, *Managerial Cost Accounting*, 4th edition (Homewood, Ill.: Richard D. Irwin, Inc., 1977), page 257.

Chapter 2

Review of the Cost Allocation Literature

The subject of indirect cost allocation has been treated extensively in the accounting literature. Most of this literature has presented logical arguments why allocations should or should not be made or how they should be made. Although some writers have reported on empirical studies of related industrial practices, very few have looked explicitly into current cost allocation practices. This study focuses on actual cost allocation practices, but it is appropriate to begin by reviewing the pertinent literature in order to set current practice in a context of widely discussed issues. As noted in the preceding chapter, three basic issues have been raised with respect to indirect cost allocations.

1. Is it feasible to make relevant and reliable allocations of indirect costs?
2. How should allocations be made?
3. For what purposes are indirect cost allocations appropriate or inappropriate?

These three issues are addressed in this sequence in the sections that follow. Logically, consideration of purposes should precede methodology in the design of a cost accounting system. However, much of the discussion of purposes in the literature is based, at least implicitly, on the assumption that methodology is known and available. The possibility of making acceptable indirect cost allocations must be considered first, of course. Much of the literature simply presumes that valid allocations are feasible. Some writers have attacked the issue directly, however. Their conclusions vary to some degree, but the consensus is clear: Indirect cost allocation is, at best, a precarious business.

Feasibility of Indirect Cost Allocation

Many authors have questioned the validity of indirect cost allocations. The most extensive and rigorous analysis of this issue has been made by Arthur L. Thomas, who has published two monographs reporting his conclusions.[1] His conclusions may be summarized quite simply: Cost allocations are arbitrary and incorrigible. Allocations are arbitrary because they are necessarily made on the basis of someone's judgment as to how they should be made and not on the basis of some logical analysis of scientific evidence. They are incorrigible (a word used here in its meaning in philosophy) because they can be neither proved correct nor rejected as incorrect. It is impossible to defend one particular allocation against all alternative possible allocations of the same cost.

For example, manufacturing overhead costs are commonly allocated to products on the basis of direct labor cost. That allocation base is chosen by management on the basis of its being reasonable, not on the basis of some well-accepted analysis that demonstrates that it is the uniquely correct allocation base. Moreover, it is impossible to prove that the resulting allocations are superior to those that would be obtained if some other measure, such as prime cost, direct labor hours, or machine hours, had been used as the allocation base. Thus, the most one can expect of allocations is that they be intuitively reasonable. Unfortunately, reasonable people may differ in their judgments on a particular allocation, and there is no way of resolving such differences other than by consent or by fiat.

With respect to cost allocations among time periods in financial reporting, Thomas suggests that the ultimate solution to the problem he identified may lie in some type of allocation-free financial statements. Statements might be based entirely on current market values or focus only on cash flows.[2] These alternatives are not examined here, as the focus of this study is not on allocations over time.

With regard to indirect cost allocations among cost objectives, Thomas offers some guidance for practical applications. Even though they are arbitrary, allocations may be useful if they are required by law or custom or if they satisfy some purpose of management in a particular organization.[3] In these cases, it is essential that allocations be "sterilized," that is, that they be made in such a way that they do not lead anyone to make an erroneous decision. Obviously, "sterile" allocations are preferable to allocations that present misleading information that may result in unwise decisions. They must still be used with caution, however, as an allocation that is "sterile" with respect to one decision may not be with respect to another. Moreover, "sterile" allocations provide no uniquely useful information; they merely prevent bad information. Allocation-free information would always be at least as useful and would require slightly less effort.[4] In summary, Thomas argues that allocations are not useful because they provide no unique information to the readers of financial reports. However, if they must be made or if management wishes to make them, at least they can be made in a way that is innocuous.

Thomas has not been alone in pointing out the dangers in common cost allocations. A study of joint costs by the National Association of Accountants noted that the problem of allocating joint costs is a universal one. Although many people tend to think of joint products and costs in connection with industries that separate basic raw materials into different products (such as oil refining), joint facilities and services and, hence, joint costs are found in virtually all industries.[5] The study then goes on to take a position that is essentially consistent with Thomas' conclusions:

> Joint costs can be allocated, but all bases for allocation imply assumptions which cannot be objectively verified. For this reason, allocations of joint costs are best avoided where not essential to the purpose for which product costs are wanted.[6]

The accounting literature is not unanimous in rejecting cost allocations, of course. Much of it focuses on why and how allocations should be made, the implicit assumption being that allocations are valid, at least under certain circumstances. Staubus argued directly in support of allocations. He said that the contention that all allocations are arbitrary is a myth. Rather, he suggested, there are good allocations and bad allocations. In general, if it is possible to measure the transfer of services from one activity to another in nonmonetary terms "with useful accuracy," it should be possible to measure the accompanying transfer of monetary value as well. In other words, this would be a good allocation. If the physical transfer of services cannot be measured, any cost allocation would be bad and should be avoided.[7]

Although Staubus' notion of a good allocation may appear to contradict Thomas' thesis, the two positions actually may be compatible. Staubus' argument could be interpreted to mean that many internal service costs that appear to be indirect are, in reality, direct costs and that reasonable transfer prices may be established for such services. In this interpretation, good allocations are really direct assignments of traceable costs, not allocations of indirect costs. If the costs allocated are opportunity costs or strictly variable costs, this line of reasoning is particularly logical.

If internal services are to be transferred at actual costs, however, and if some of those costs are fixed, one again faces an inescapably arbitrary allocation problem. The special problem of fixed costs in this context is well expressed in a research report on the costs of productive capacity.

> Underlying the allocation process is an implicit assumption that the amount of cost being allocated varies with the number of basis units contained in the period's production or sales. Where the amount of cost assigned to the period is independent of the number of basis units reported during the period (i.e., where the cost is fixed), the resulting unit cost is determined by arbitrary decision or accidental occurrence rather than by predictable cause-and-effect relationships.[8]

This study accepts the fact that cost allocations *are* made. It does not seek to convince the reader that they should or should not be made. Rather, it seeks to determine how and why allocations are made. The remainder of this chapter addresses answers to these questions that have been offered in the accounting literature.

Methodology of Indirect Cost Allocation

The methodology of cost allocation has two principal issues: What separate pools of indirect costs should be identified and allocated together? Over what base should the costs in any given pool be allocated? Both of these issues, but particularly the latter, depend upon the objective of allocation. Furthermore, the objective should lead to the specification of a criterion or criteria for the choice of an allocation method.

If the purpose of a particular allocation is simply to satisfy some broadly worded external requirement, management is likely to establish only a few broad indirect cost pools and to allocate them over any readily available bases. In effect, the criterion for choosing allocation methods in this case is convenience. If the requirement is not specific and if management has little interest in the allocations, it is only natural that the easiest acceptable methods will be chosen. On the other hand, if management has some explicit objective of its own, such as to use allocations to induce a particular pattern of behavior by division managers, there are likely to be more indirect cost pools, comprising groups of homogeneous cost items, and more carefully selected allocation bases.

As we mentioned earlier, the issues of the composition of an indirect cost pool and the allocation base are not unrelated. Indeed, one reason for combining a particular set of costs in one pool is that a single allocation base is reasonable for all those costs. The Cost Accounting Standards Board, which tended to favor more rather than fewer cost pools, recognized that otherwise unlike costs may be grouped in a single pool if a common allocation base would be appropriate for all of them in any case.[9] (The CASB terminated operations on September 30, 1980.) To the extent that the literature deals with methodology issues, it usually focuses on the allocation base rather than on the composition of the indirect cost pool. This emphasis is reasonable since the allocation base may be the principal determinant of the composition of the pool.

The choice of allocation methodology should follow from the definition of objectives and consistent criteria. Much of the literature on methodology has addressed criteria rather than specific cost pools and allocation bases. As will be seen in the discussions that follow, some criteria are so vague that they are of little practical assistance in a specific situation.

Fairness or Equity

This is an intuitively appealing criterion. No one would argue for unfairness or inequity. Fairness, or equity, has been identified as the basic criterion for allocating costs to defense contracts.[10] The obvious difficulty with this criterion is its inherently subjective nature. For example, division managers may disagree with corporate management about what is a "fair" share of corporate expenses to be allocated to their divisions, even though both parties agree that "fairness" is critical to the allocation.

Benefit

One frequently reads that indirect costs should be allocated among cost objectives in proportion to the benefits that those cost objectives receive from the services for which the indirect costs are incurred. Although benefit is a somewhat more operational criterion than fairness, it, too, depends on human judgment in most cases, and it becomes increasingly difficult to apply as the services become more remote from the cost objectives.[11] Some assumption must be made about the beneficial relationship between an indirect cost and the benefiting cost objectives, and "equally tenable assumptions as to the incidence of benefits may yield quite different costs for the same" cost objective.[12]

Benefit is probably a viable criterion when the connection between the cost and the cost objective is easily seen in the form of some physical good or measurable service. For example, there may be no disagreement that factory departments benefit from a power plant in proportion to their consumptions of power. However, there may be no agreement as to how those same departments benefit from the factory manager's office staff.

Cause

It is intuitively reasonable that indirect costs should be allocated in proportion to whatever factor or factors cause those costs—if those causal factors are clearly identifiable in the cost objectives to which the allocation is to be made. For example, a factory maintenance department's costs might be allocated among other departments in proportion to the maintenance work done in those departments. Such an allocation base is particularly satisfactory if the costs to be allocated are wholly or largely variable with the volume of work done. The presence of substantial amounts of fixed costs makes cause less attractive as an allocation criterion because fixed costs are directly attributable to a decision to provide a given level of service capacity and not to the volume of use of the service.[13]

There seems to be some question on the relationship between benefit and cause as allocation criteria. The Cost Accounting Standards Board indicated that costs should be allocated on the basis of the "beneficial or causal relationship" between them and the cost objectives.[14] However, it did not specify whether it viewed benefit and cause as synonymous or as alternatives, each applicable under different circumstances. The Boeing Company has argued that benefit and cause are not conflicting alternatives but, rather, parallel and inherently related notions. It contended that benefit is the purpose of every cost and should be considered in allocating it. Furthermore, the cause of a cost is simply a reflection of the relationship between that cost and the cost objectives that benefit from it.[15]

There has been considerable controversy on this point in connection with the allocation of state and local taxes to defense contracts. The government has argued that these taxes should be allocated on the basis of the factors that cause their incurrence by the taxpayer. For example, Lockheed Aircraft Corporation paid property tax on inventories used for commercial contracts only, not on inventories for government contracts. Consequently, the government contended that the tax should be allocated to commercial business only, not to government contracts. Lockheed responded that the tax funded public services were provided uniformly to the corporation and to its employees and, thus, that all work benefited proportionately from those public services and the tax paid to support them. The Court of Claims accepted Lockheed's argument in this case but cautioned that it did so only in the particular circumstances of the case and was not making a general rule applicable to all taxes.[16]

Neutrality

This is a criterion that is particularly favored by writers who question the validity of indirect cost allocations to begin with. It is essentially the same as the notion of "sterility" that Thomas suggested when arbitrary allocations were to be made.[17] The neutrality criterion is intended to lead to the choice of allocation methods that avoid misleading information and, thus, prevent inappropriate decisions and inefficient disputes. The difficulty, again, is that a method that is neutral with respect to one decision may not be so with respect to some other decision.

Moriarity proposed an allocation method that is neutral with respect to the decision on whether to provide a service jointly to two or more segments of a firm or to allow each segment to buy the service separately. He reasoned that every service can be purchased separately by segments at some price and, thus, the primary reason for joint services and their joint costs must be that they are cheaper than the separate alternatives. Common services are provided and common costs are incurred only because they entail some net cost savings.

Moriarity recommended, then, that the indirect costs of common services be allocated by first charging each segment with the cost of obtaining its own services separately and then crediting each segment with a share of the total cost saving from the common service in proportion to its separate costs. In this way, the cost allocated to any segment is always equal to or less than the cost of its next best alternative (its separate costs). Thus, the segment would have no incentive to seek to obtain the service separately. Moriarity noted that this neutral allocation method has the additional advantage of fairness, in that all segments share in the costs of and the cost savings from the common services.[18]

Independence of Cost Objectives

This criterion asserts that the allocation method should be designed so that the amount of cost allocated to one cost objective is not affected by actions or events in other cost objectives during the period for which the allocation is made.[19] This is a criterion that is particularly important when the objective of the cost allocation is an evaluation of performances in individual cost objectives, such as segments of a firm.

Ability to Bear

This criterion is usually suggested only as a last alternative, when nothing better can be found. It states that costs should be allocated in proportion to cost objectives' abilities to bear the charge for those costs. In effect, it leads to allocation on the basis of some measure of the size of the cost objectives. The premise is that bigger cost objectives can afford to bear larger shares of indirect costs. Obviously, it is a criterion unrelated to any explicit notion of benefit, cause, neutrality, or independence. It was the Cost Accounting Standards Board's criterion for allocating costs that exhibit no beneficial or causal relationship to cost objectives.[20] The Board, of course, was concerned with a context in which laws and regulations require that indirect costs be fully allocated. When allocation is not mandatory and no better criterion than ability to bear is applicable, a good argument can be made that no allocation at all should be made.

The foregoing six criteria recur in the literature, but they do not necessarily resolve the questions of methodology in the allocation of indirect costs. It is one thing to state a reasonable-sounding criterion, but it is quite another to translate it into an unambiguous allocation in a specific situation. Skousen, while recommending that all costs be allocated among segments for financial reporting, recognized that criteria had to be established before management could choose acceptable allocation bases in accordance with those criteria. He concluded that considerable research was necessary before any such criteria could be established.[21] Unfortunately, much of the literature causes one to wonder whether such research can ever be truly fruitful. To date, there is little evidence that accountants might agree on how various criteria interact with each other or on how to determine which criterion is dominant in a particular situation.

Objectives of Indirect Cost Allocation

The remainder of this review of the cost allocation literature is organized according to the four basic objectives of allocation that were identified in the preceding chapter:

1. Financial reporting

2. Planning and decision making
3. Pricing
4. Control and performance evaluation

Cost Allocations for Financial Reporting

Allocations of indirect costs among cost objectives are particularly important in financial reporting in two contexts: the valuation of inventories of manufactured products and the reporting of segment earnings. With regard to inventory valuation, the two major issues discussed in the literature have been the nature of the costs that should be included in inventory and the methods by which indirect costs should be allocated among different items of inventory. These issues have been treated at considerable length in the accounting literature and have been well summarized in a variety of cost accounting texts. Hence, they will be reviewed only briefly here.

In general, the literature indicates that costs of manufacturing or production are product costs and, therefore, should be charged to inventory. Costs of other functions, such as selling and administration, are usually regarded as period costs, to be charged directly to expense in the period in which they are incurred. The principal authoritative pronouncement on this matter is found in Chapter 4 of Accounting Research Bulletin No. 43.

> As applied to inventories, cost means in principle the sum of the applicable expenditures and charges directly *or indirectly* incurred in bringing an article to its existing condition and location.[22] (Emphasis added.)

The statement goes on to note some of the difficulties that may be encountered in allocating certain costs to inventories. For example, certain production costs, such as the costs of idle facilities and excessive spoilage, may not be properly allocable to inventory. Furthermore, although general and administrative expenses should normally be treated as period costs, such expenses that are clearly related to production should be included in inventory. The most explicit statement with respect to indirect costs is that the exclusion of all overhead from inventory is unacceptable. The statement concludes by noting the need for judgment in the individual situation.[23] That such judgment is, indeed, exercised is reflected in the responses to a survey of inventory allocation practices in 1,200 companies. Forty-four percent indicated that they allocated "all expenditures that are indirectly related to production" to inventories in external financial statements, and 56% replied that they did not.[24]

Another aspect of the issue regarding the nature of costs to be included in inventory is the treatment of fixed manufacturing overhead. This, of course, is one of the central features of the debate over absorption costing and direct costing. Although direct costing does not exclude all overhead from inventory, it does exclude a significant portion—fixed overhead. The excerpt from Accounting Research Bulletin No. 43 quoted above is not absolutely clear on this point, but it has been widely cited as prohibiting the use of direct costing in external financial reports.[25] Presumably, direct costing would be especially appealing to those who are frustrated by the need for arbitrary allocations, because it avoids the more difficult allocation to inventory—the allocation of fixed costs.

Authoritative pronouncements have given little attention to methods of indirect cost allocation for financial reporting purposes. The literature of cost accounting has included a great many discussions of methodology, however. Most of these discussions explain allocation methods and the circumstances under which they are most appropriate. There has been no substantial effort to standardize allocation methodology or to advance one allocation base as superior to all others. The authors of one cost accounting text, for example, present six different allocation bases and note some advantages and disadvantages of each. They offer no comments on the overall preferability of the alternatives, however. They simply note that each may be applicable under different production conditions.[26]

Indirect cost allocations for purposes of segment reporting are a relatively recent requirement in financial reporting. Statement of Financial Accounting Standards No. 14 requires the reporting of operating profit or loss for "reportable segments." Indirect costs are specifically required to be allocated among these segments.

> . . . those operating expenses . . . that are not directly traceable to an industry segment shall be allocated *on a reasonable basis* among those industry segments *for whose benefit* the expenses were incurred.[27] (Emphasis added.)

The intended criterion for allocation obviously is "benefit," but the method of allocation is left to the management of the individual firm. No further guidance is offered as to what constitutes "a reasonable basis." It is clear, however, that the Financial Accounting Standards Board believed that indirect cost allocations were not so arbitrary as to be useless. The earlier exposure draft of this particular statement would have required firms to report both profit contribution before and operating profit after indirect cost allocations. In the final version, however, the requirement of profit contribution was omitted. Firms may elect to report the contribution before allocation of common costs, but they are still required to present the operating profit after such allocation.[28]

Others have taken a less favorable view of segment earnings computed after indirect cost allocations. A research report summarizing the views of financial analysts, bankers, and corporate executives concluded that "segment contributions to common costs and profit" were both relevant to users of financial statements and reliable, but that the presence of common costs tended to invalidate net earnings figures for segments.[29]

In another study, investors indicated that net profit figures for segments lost significance when common costs allocated to those segments exceeded some percentage of segment sales revenue. Twenty-seven percent of these respondents stated that this critical percentage of sales was 5% or less, and 63% of the investors questioned said that the critical level was 10% of sales or less.[30] The same study sought to determine the percentage of total common costs to total corporate sales in diversified companies. Seventy-three percent of the companies surveyed reported common costs equal to or greater than 5% of sales, whereas 36% indicated that their common costs exceeded 10% of sales.[31]

Caution must be used in attempting to relate the percentages in these two sets of responses. Investors were asked about the percentage of common costs to sales in individual segments, whereas the companies were asked to indicate the percentage of common costs to sales in the entire corporation. Nevertheless, these two sets of data do show that common costs are potentially material amounts in diversified corporations and that investors are concerned about the impact that they have on the validity of reported segment earnings. Rappaport and Lerner noted the findings of this preceding study of segment reporting and concluded that, because

> . . . arbitrary allocations of common costs may obscure important relationships between revenues and earnings, it is recommended that all common expenses be treated as corporate expenses rather than allocated to individual segments.[32]

Cost Allocations for Planning and Decision Making

The essential role that cost data play in planning and decision making is to assist managers in predicting or estimating what costs will be in the future as a consequence of the plans or decisions under consideration. Thus, the emphasis must be on estimates of future costs that will be affected by plans or decisions made now. Such costs are commonly referred to as incremental costs or differential costs. Obviously, historical costs are not directly relevant for decision making, although they may be useful bases for estimating future costs. Similarly, costs charged to cost objectives, whether traced directly or allocated, are not relevant if the decision or plan is not framed in terms of those cost objectives.

Relevant cost data are those that are expected to be uniquely associated with the consequences of a specific plan or decision. Such cost data must be developed within the context of that specific decision. No routine system of cost allocation can be relied upon to provide the appropriate information for every different decision problem that is encountered. Hence, the clear consensus of the literature is that cost allocations, as such, are not useful for planning or decision making.

Many writers distinguish between short-run and long-run decision situations. In the short run, decisions will be made within the constraint of existing capacity and the related costs. Thus, the relevant costs are usually variable costs and small increments of fixed costs. Conventional allocations of full costs are unlikely to be good estimators of these short-run incremental costs.

In the long run, however, plans and decisions may involve changes in capacity and in fixed costs generally. The relevant costs are the incremental long-run costs in the particular situation. In many cases, these incremental long-run costs may be difficult to estimate. The plans under consideration are complex and are likely to interact with other plans affecting the long run in a manner that is hard to predict. Consequently, many writers have suggested that allocations of indirect costs at the level currently being incurred may be the best available estimates of long-run incremental costs.[33] In such a case, the allocations of indirect costs are not relevant *per se*. Rather, they are useful surrogates for the truly relevant but elusive long-run incremental costs.

Cost Allocations for Pricing

In economic theory, the costs that are relevant to pricing are opportunity costs. Conceptually, these are not the same as the actual, standard, and budgeted costs that are commonly available in accounting records and reports. In particular situations, accounting cost data may be the best available estimates of opportunity costs; but management cannot rely on this to be true generally. Full costs, including allocations of indirect costs, are likely to be particularly poor estimators of opportunity costs in short-run pricing situations. In the long run, full costs may have more value as estimators.[34]

In any case, the role of costs in pricing in economic theory is to determine supply, both for the market as a whole and for the individual seller, not to determine prices directly. In pure competition, prices are established by the interaction of supply and demand in the market. The individual seller has no discretion; it accepts the market price as given. If a single firm has costs below normal for the industry, its advantage will be short-lived, as competitors will promptly bid up the price for whatever factor of production gives the firm its cost advantage. Conversely, if one firm's costs are above normal for the industry, it must either reduce them or eventually go out of business. It cannot raise its own prices to compensate for its higher costs.[35]

In the case of a monopoly, a market in which there is only one seller, the individual seller's costs are the entire market's costs and, hence, determine total market supply. In an unregulated monopoly, prices are set by the interaction between the single seller's supply and market demand. Government has demonstrated a marked tendency to regulate monopolies, however. This regulation is usually designed to establish a price that is "fair" to both the seller and its customers.

Public utilities are classic examples of regulated monopolies. Prices in regulated monopolies are usually established on the basis of the seller's estimated costs plus some target profit or rate of return on investment. Essentially the same pricing policy is applied to cost-type defense contracts, except that prices are more likely to be based on actual costs, as measured and reported in the accounting system. Moreover, these costs include full allocations of all indirect costs.[36]

Since indirect cost allocations are necessary for the determination of regulated prices, it is not surprising that the regulators should establish rules for the methods of allocation used. Those methods will partially determine the prices to be paid. Most of the standards promulgated by the Cost Accounting Standards Board deal in some way with indirect costs and their allocation. Indeed, it is probably true that the Board would not have been created by the U.S. Congress if it were not for problems associated with indirect costs.[37]

The most complex situation in which cost allocations may play a role in the determination of prices is in imperfectly competitive markets. In these markets, there is an element of competition from other sellers but also an element of price discretion allowed to each individual seller. Each firm sells a product that is different in some way, however slight, from the products of competitors. That degree of product differentiation permits the seller to manipulate its price within some range without fear of retaliation by competitors or loss of customers to them. Within this range of price discretion, the individual firm's costs may be used to establish the price.

Exactly how costs help to determine prices is not entirely clear, however. Often, costs are used to establish initial target prices, but management may then deviate from those prices to cope with market forces or with other considerations, such as the danger of increased competition in the long run or the threat of regulation.[38] Consequently, indirect cost allocations are, at most, parts of one phase of the pricing process in imperfectly competitive markets. Their inherently subjective nature suggests that they should be viewed as reflections of management's goal of full cost recovery in pricing and not as processes that lead to a precise determination of product costs and, hence, prices.[39]

In other words, indirect cost allocations may play some role in the development of prices in imperfect markets, but the exact nature of that role cannot be generalized. It probably varies from firm to firm and from time to time. It is a tenuous role, at best. The uncertainty here is well reflected in the following conclusion regarding the role of allocations in the pricing of joint products:

> . . . if established market prices are lacking, a seller has more scope for independent pricing action and product costs are usually wanted as a guide to pricing. Here joint costs are allocated to products in proportions reflecting the manner in which management wishes to recover the costs in selling prices. However, customer willingness to pay must be kept in mind.[40]

Cost Allocations for Control and Performance Evaluation

One of the most complex and controversial questions with respect to indirect cost allocations is whether they are useful in stimulating managers to control costs and evaluating managers' cost control performance. Answers to this question in the literature run the gamut between both extremes. Some writers have argued that allocations are useful for cost control and performance measurement, and others have contended that allocations actually interfere with effective control and performance assessments. A third group has concluded that the answer depends upon the situation and the attitudes of the managers involved.

One point on which there is general agreement is that indirect costs are not traceable to individual cost objectives and, therefore, that the amounts of costs allocated cannot be expected to be avoided if the cost objectives are eliminated. For example, arbitrary allocations of truly common costs among products can make certain products appear to be unprofitable. Yet, if such products were discontinued, total corporate profit would be reduced. Thus, the profits or losses reported for individual products after allocations are not reliable measures of those products' profit performances.[41] This situation leads some writers to conclude that allocations should not be made.[42] Others, however, conclude simply that it is important that allocations be clearly labeled as such in performance reports and that they not be included in computations of incentive compensations.[43]

Even though allocated costs would not be avoided if a particular cost objective were eliminated, is it still possible that the allocation will in some way facilitate management's control of those costs? Elimination of a cost objective would be the result of a decision, of course, and only incremental cost data would be relevant to the decision analysis. However, if management wishes to evaluate the cost objective on an ongoing basis, are only the same incremental costs relevant?

The literature is divided on this question. On the one hand is the view that costs can be controlled only at their source, that is, in the responsibility center in which they are initially incurred.[44] In this view, allocations are not helpful because they are affected by factors unrelated to managerial performance in the cost objective to which the allocations are made. Moreover, they distract management's attention from the total amounts of costs that can be controlled and divert it, unproductively, to methods of allocation.[45]

The opposite view is that cost control requires management to be aware of all costs. Thus, while final allocations of indirect costs to products may not help in cost control, intermediate allocations to other responsibility centers (for example, from service centers to production departments) do help. In this view, many, if not most, indirect costs involve joint responsibility, and it is better to make cost allocations based on only partial responsibility or on overlapping responsibilities than to leave costs unallocated at their source.[46]

A middle position on the usefulness of allocations for control and performance evaluation is that it depends on the individual managers involved. Allocations may be beneficial to the cost control initiative of some and detrimental to the initiative of others. Moreover, one method of allocation may have a beneficial effect for certain costs but not for others. Thus, the design of a system of allocations for control purposes will be very difficult and will require frequent reviews to prevent undesirable behavioral reactions by managers.[47]

If cost allocations are useful in appraising managers' cost control efforts, there seems to be agreement that it is because of the motivational effect that they have on managers rather than because of any inherent economic validity of the allocations. The positive view of allocations for this purpose is frequently expressed as a need to make managers aware that indirect costs exist and must be covered by the direct profit contributions of the segments if the firm as a whole is to be profitable and survive.[48] However, it may be necessary for top management to "sell" allocations to segment managers, particularly when new indirect cost categories are created or when indirect costs are increased substantially for any reason or methods of allocation are changed.[49]

Bodnar and Lusk have suggested that indirect cost allocations can be designed expressly to reinforce managers' motivation to achieve some specified goal, even if the methods of allocation appear illogical for other purposes. Their suggestion is that alternative possible allocation bases be identified and that segments' performances be measured according to each of these. Whichever base best reinforces the desired performance is the one to be used in performance reporting.

The example they offered was that of a university that wished to emphasize publications by its faculty. Use of the library was assumed to be correlated positively with numbers of publications. Thus, to stimulate publications, the department whose faculty published the most would be allocated the smallest share of library costs, and the one with the least publications would receive the largest allocation.[50] This particular method would not motivate department heads to control library costs, of course, but it would encourage them to strive to have their departments accomplish the overall goal of the university. It should be noted also that this method violates the criterion of independence that was mentioned earlier. Better publication performance by one department would tend to increase the library costs allocated to others.

Some authors have argued that allocations of indirect costs of central services to segments stimulate segment managers to control those costs in two ways. First, the segment managers are encouraged to use central services only to the extent that they are actually economical for the segment. If no allocation is made, a segment manager will regard a central service as free and, consequently, may tend to use it excessively. As a result, the total cost of the central service may be increased and other segments may incur unnecessary costs because of delays due to overuse of the service. Although the amounts of indirect costs allocated may not be accurate measures of these additional unnecessary costs, they may be acceptable surrogates for the real costs and clearly preferable to an inference that there is no cost associated with the central services.

The second way in which segment managers may seek to control indirect costs in response to allocations is by putting pressure on the managers of service centers to control the costs originating in their centers. In other words, segment managers are more likely to complain about high service costs if they are allocated to their segments and appear on their performance reports. Thus, segment managers may be stimulated to control indirect costs both by controlling their own usage of the related services and by pressuring responsible service center managers to control the costs for which they are responsible.[51]

In a survey of practices regarding allocations of corporate expenses to divisions, firms that did not make such allocations tended to disagree with the logic of the foregoing arguments. They contended that allocations violate the concept of decentralization and also weaken a sense of cost responsibility in the corporate office, where the allocated expenses must be controlled. Furthermore, they indicated that they felt segment managers could do nothing constructive to control the allocated expenses.[52] Presumably, complaining to corporate managers was not regarded as a constructive activity.

With regard to the question of segment managers controlling indirect costs by controlling their own volumes of use of services, there may be a difference in implicit assumptions. Those who favor that view may be assuming either that the costs involved are variable with usage or that the demand for central services exceeds a service capacity constraint. Those who reject this view may presume that the indirect costs are essentially fixed and that capacity is not a problem. In reality, of course, both conditions may exist in the same firm. Central data processing services, for example, might entail substantially variable costs and might be subject to a real capacity constraint. Corporate executives' salaries, on the other hand, are fixed costs that are not related to any readily measurable notion of capacity. Generalizations about all indirect costs may be dangerous.

Notes

1. Arthur L. Thomas, *The Allocation Problem in Financial Accounting Theory*. Studies in Accounting Research No. 3 (Evanston, Ill.: American Accounting Association, 1969) and *The Allocation Problem: Part Two*. Studies in Accounting Research No. 9 (Sarasota, Fla.: American Accounting Association, 1974).

2. Arthur L. Thomas, *The Allocation Problem: Part Two, op. cit.*, Chapter 7.

3. Arthur L. Thomas, "Useful Arbitrary Allocations," *The Accounting Review*, XLVI (July 1971), page 474.

4. Arthur L. Thomas, *The Allocation Problem: Part Two, op. cit.*, pages 40–46.

5. *Costing Joint Products*. Research Series No. 31 (New York: National Association of Accountants, 1957), page 1.

6. *Ibid.*, page 2.

7. George J. Staubus, *Activity Costing and Input–Output Accounting* (Homewood, Ill.: Richard D. Irwin, Inc., 1971), pages 142–143.

8. *Accounting for Costs of Capacity*. Research Report No. 39 (New York: National Association of Accountants, 1963), page 46.

9. *Restatement of Objectives, Policies and Concepts* (Washington, D.C.: Cost Accounting Standards Board, 1977), pages 6–7.

10. *Ibid.*, page 3, and *Defense Acquisition Regulations*, Section 15-201.1.

11. Howard W. Wright and James P. Bedingfield, "Benefit as a Criterion for Indirect Cost Allocation," *The Federal Accountant*, XXII (September 1973), page 68.

12. *Accounting for Costs of Capacity, op. cit.*, page 61.

13. Charles T. Horngren, *Cost Accounting: A Managerial Emphasis*, 4th edition (Englewood Cliffs, N.J.: Prentice-Hall, Inc., 1977), page 499.

14. *Restatement of Objectives, Policies and Concepts, op. cit.*, pages 5–8.

15. *Towards Common Concepts of Cost Allocations in Cost Accounting* (Seattle, Wash.: The Boeing Company, 1978), pages 45–46.

16. Wright and Bedingfield, *op. cit.*, page 70.

17. Thomas, *The Allocation Problem: Part Two, op. cit.*, pages 40–46.

18. Shane Moriarity, "Another Approach to Allocating Joint Costs," *The Accounting Review*, L (October 1975), pages 791–795. A somewhat similar proposal is presented in Daniel L. Jensen, "A Class of Mutually Satisfactory Allocations," *The Accounting Review*, LII (October 1977), pages 842–856.

19. Horngren, *op. cit.*, page 501, and David Solomons, *Divisional Performance: Measurement and Control* (Homewood, Ill.: Richard D. Irwin, Inc., 1965), page 67.

20. *Restatement of Objectives, Policies and Concepts, op. cit.*, page 8.

21. K. Fred Skousen, "A Format for Reporting Segment Profits," *Management Accounting*, LII (June 1971), page 19.

22. *Accounting Research and Terminology Bulletins: Final Edition* (New York: American Institute of Certified Public Accountants, 1961), page 28.

23. *Ibid.*, page 29.

24. Stephen Landekich, "Cost Allocations to Inventory," *Management Accounting*, LIV (March 1973), page 51.

25. An extensive review of the literature on direct costing may be found in Charles Weber, *The Evolution of Direct Costing* (Urbana: University of Illinois, 1966).

26. John J. W. Neuner and Edward B. Deakin III, *Cost Accounting: Principles and Practices*, 9th edition (Homewood, Ill.: Richard D. Irwin, Inc., 1977), pages 213–216.

27. *Financial Reporting for Segments of a Business Enterprise*. Statement of Financial Accounting Standards No. 14 (Stamford, Conn.: Financial Accounting Standards Board, 1976), paragraph 10.d, page 6.

28. *Ibid.*, paragraph 78, pages 35–36.

29. Morton Backer and Walter B. McFarland, *External Reporting for Segments of a Business* (New York: National Association of Accountants, 1968), pages 15–16 and 100.

30. R. K. Mautz, *Financial Reporting by Diversified Companies* (New York: Financial Executives Research Foundation, 1968), page 309.

31. *Ibid.*, page 227.

32. Alfred Rappaport and Eugene M. Lerner, *Segment Reporting for Managers and Investors* (New York: National Association of Accountants, 1972), page 46.

33. Robert N. Anthony and Glenn A. Welsch, *Fundamentals of Management Accounting*, revised edition (Homewood, Ill.: Richard D. Irwin, Inc., 1977) page 259; Horngren, *op. cit.*, pages 502–503; James E. Joyce, "The Overhead Mystique," *Management Accounting*, L (November 1968), pages 43–46; and Gordon Shillinglaw, *Managerial Cost Accounting*, 4th edition (Homewood, Ill.: Richard D. Irwin, Inc., 1977), pages 257–260.

34. "Product Costs for Pricing Purposes," *N.A.C.A. Bulletin*, XXXIV (August 1953), pages 1708–1729.

35. The economic theory of pricing in competitive markets is expounded in detail in a wide range of economics texts. See, for example, James R. McGuigan and R. Charles Moyer, *Managerial Economics* (Hinsdale, Ill.: The Dryden Press, 1975), pages 306–313.

36. *Restatement of Objectives, Policies and Concepts, op. cit.*, page 5.

37. Comptroller General of the United States, *Report on the Feasibility of Applying Uniform Cost-Accounting Standards to Negotiated Defense Contracts* (Washington, D.C.: U.S. Government Printing Office, 1970), pages 17–19, 51–65, and 71–101.

38. *Accounting for Costs of Capacity, op. cit.*, page 60.

39. *Ibid.*, page 5.

40. *Costing Joint Products, op. cit.*, page 5.

41. *Accounting for Costs of Capacity, op. cit.*, pages 46–47.

42. David Solomons, *Divisional Performance: Measurement and Control* (Homewood, Ill.: Richard D. Irwin, Inc., 1965), pages 72–73.

43. Carl G. Baumes, *Allocating Corporate Expenses*. Business Policy Study No. 108 (New York: National Industrial Conference Board, Inc., 1963), page 69.

44. John A. Beckett, "A Study of the Principles of Allocating Costs," *The Accounting Review*, XXVI (July 1951), pages 328–329, and James M. Fremgen, *Accounting for Managerial Analysis*, 3rd edition (Homewood, Ill.: Richard D. Irwin, Inc., 1976), page 121.

45. *Costing Joint Products*, *op. cit.*, page 51.

46. R. Lee Brummet, *Overhead Costing* (Ann Arbor: University of Michigan, 1957), pages 140–142.

47. Mautz, *op. cit.*, pages 27–28.

48. Baumes, *op. cit.*, page 6.

49. *Ibid.*, page 69.

50. George Bodnar and Edward J. Lusk, "Motivational Considerations in Cost Allocation Systems: A Conditioning Theory Approach," *The Accounting Review*, LII (October 1977), pages 857–868.

51. Baumes, *op. cit.*, pages 6–9, and Jerold L. Zimmerman, "The Costs and Benefits of Cost Allocations," *The Accounting Review*, LIV (July 1979), pages 504–521.

52. Baumes, op. cit., pages 81–84.

Chapter 3

An Analysis of Indirect Cost Allocation Practices

Although the allocation of indirect costs has been the subject of extensive discussions in the accounting literature, most of those discussions are conceptual in nature and are limited to arguments about why allocations should or should not be made. Few studies have looked explicitly at actual allocation practices. In order to address the issue of indirect cost allocation, one must consider the following four questions:

1. Which costs are considered indirect?
2. Which indirect costs are allocated to profit centers?
3. How are allocations made?
4. Why are allocations made or not made?

This chapter reports the results of a questionnaire survey and follow-up interviews dealing with the first two questions above. The next two chapters present the results of the same survey regarding the third and fourth questions.

Statistical Method Used in Analysis of Different Practices

The statistical technique used in this chapter to analyze the differences in indirect cost allocation practices among different groups of companies is the chi-square test. In analyzing the number of respondents treating indirect costs in certain ways, one can classify the respondents according to various relevant characteristics, such as size or industry, and present the results of the analysis in separate sets of frequencies or percentages for the different classes of respondents. The chi-square test is then used to determine whether the differences among two or more sets of data are truly significant or are attributable merely to chance.

A chi-square value is computed from the differences in frequencies or percentages in the different sets of data. If two sets of data are identical, the value of chi-square will be zero. On the other hand, if there are significant differences between the two sets of data, the resultant chi-square value will be large. Thus, a low value of chi-square means that different sets of data are essentially similar and differences among them are merely random variations. Conversely, a high value of chi-square indicates that the differences among different sets of data are significant.

The level of statistical significance of the differences among different sets of data is not determined by the chi-square value alone. It depends also on the number of sets of data (such as different industries) and the number of variables in each set (such as different allocation practices), or the so-called degrees of freedom. The higher the degrees of freedom, the greater the differences among different sets of data must be before those differences are considered significant at a given level. Therefore, it is the level of significance, not the chi-square value itself, that is useful in interpreting differences in indirect cost allocation practices among different groups of firms.

Given a chi-square value and the degrees of freedom associated with observed differences in allocation practices among two or more groups of firms, one refers to the standard chi-square table to determine a level of significance stated as a percentage or probability. For example, if a chi-square value is found to be statistically significant at the 1% level, it means that there is only one chance in a hundred that the differences in indirect cost allocation practices among different groups of respondents are random variations attributable merely to chance. Conversely, there are 99 chances in 100 that the differences are significant.

In this study, the conventional 5% level of statistical significance is used as the upper limit for classifying differences as significant. If differences in practices among firms with different demographic characteristics are not statistically significant at the 5% level, at least, only summary data for all respondents are reported in the sections that follow. If differences significant at the 5% level or lower are observed, however, responses from the different groups of firms are reported separately, and the level of statistical significance is indicated.

Nature of Indirect Costs

Most of the controversy over indirect cost allocation has focused on the allocation issue in general, without examining the treatments of individual cost items. Analyzing the components of indirect cost pools and the extent of their allocation may shed some light on the basic issue. Therefore, it seems appropriate to examine the nature of corporate indirect costs before discussing cost allocation practices.

In any enterprise consisting of a number of segments, or profit centers, there are, unavoidably, certain costs that are common to two or more of the segments. At a minimum, the costs of operating the corporate administrative offices are incurred to some extent for the benefit of all the segments. Since the costs are common to more than one segment, they cannot be associated in their entirety with any single segment. This relationship is in contrast to direct costs, which are incurred solely for or within one segment of a company.

It is difficult to question the literal truth of the argument that indirect costs common to two or more segments of a company can be allocated among those segments only on some arbitrary basis. However, it should be recognized that the acceptability of different arbitrary allocations may vary substantially. In some cases, it may be entirely reasonable to allocate indirect costs to segments, despite some degree of arbitrariness in the allocation procedure. In other cases, no allocation may appear reasonable. Whether it is reasonable to allocate indirect costs depends on the nature of those costs.

The respondents to the survey reported here clearly distinguished between two types of indirect costs at the corporate level: corporate administrative costs and corporate service costs. Corporate administrative costs are the expenses of maintaining a corporate entity and a central office. Corporate executives' compensation, institutional advertising, and corporate legal services are examples. Such expenses are necessary costs of operating the company as a separate legal entity. Corporate service costs, on the other hand, are the expenses of providing services that could either be performed separately in each profit center or be centralized at the corporate level, presumably in the interest of greater efficiency. Data processing, accounting, personnel functions, and research and development are good examples. However, few corporate service costs are caused exclusively by the segments or profit centers. Centralized services are typically performed for the firm as an entity as well as for its segments. Thus, virtually all corporate service costs include some elements of corporate administrative costs. The accounting function, for example, could be performed in each operating segment, but the central office would still need a small staff to consolidate the segments' financial statements.

Although corporate service costs often can be traced to some extent to the activities of individual operating segments, they are still indirect costs because the services are performed centrally for several segments and because they include significant amounts of fixed costs necessary to provide a given level of service capacity. Some firms do consider these service costs as direct because of their traceability to segments, while others treat them as indirect because they are incurred centrally. How various specific corporate expenses are classified by survey respondents will be discussed later in this chapter. One thing is clear at the outset, however. Corporate service costs were clearly distinguished from corporate administrative costs and were treated differently by most firms.

This distinction between corporate service costs and administrative costs seems to shed some light on the question of the relationship between benefit and cause as allocation criteria. The term "causal or beneficial relationship" is found in the literature. However, as noted in the preceding chapter, it is not clear whether cause and benefit should be viewed as synonyms or as alternatives. In light of the distinction between corporate service costs and administrative costs, it seems reasonable to conclude that cause and benefit are alternatives and not a single criterion.

Corporate service costs are incurred mainly because of demand from segments or profit centers. Thus, the costs are caused by the operations of the segments. Corporate administrative costs, on the other hand, are not incurred by actions of segments but by the mere existence of the corporate entity. Every segment benefits from corporate administration in that it is relieved of the need to perform the administrative functions itself, but it is impossible to measure the benefits received by each segment objectively.

One may argue that benefit is inherent in every service cost caused by a profit center and, therefore, that cause necessarily implies benefit. There is still a basic difference between cause and benefit, however. A causal relationship lends itself to reasonably objective measurement, whereas a beneficial relationship does not. This difference is reflected in the results of the questionnaire survey and in the in-depth interviews. Most executives interviewed felt strongly that corporate service costs should be allocated to profit centers because the centers are the main causes of the costs and are properly charged for them. These executives' feelings about allocating corporate administrative costs were somewhat mixed, however, and when allocations were made, their validity frequently was questioned.

The distinction between corporate service costs and corporate administrative costs and the different reactions to allocations of these two types of cost seem compatible with Staubus' contention (discussed in Chapter 2) that there are good allocations and bad allocations.[1] Since the transfer of corporate services can be measured in nonmonetary quantities with "useful accuracy," the parallel allocation of the service costs is good. As no similar physical transfer can be observed for corporate administration, however, any allocations of the related costs would be bad.

Indirect costs similar to corporate administrative costs and service costs also exist at every level of managerial responsibility in a company with a hierarchy of organizational components. This study addresses only the indirect costs incurred at the corporate level, since indirect costs incurred at lower levels of responsibility are often subject to differing allocation policies set by the several division managements.

Amount of Indirect Costs at the Corporate Level

The relative amounts of indirect costs incurred at the corporate level varied significantly among the survey respondents. They ranged from as low as 0.02% to as high as 44% of sales (net operating revenue in banks and premiums in insurance companies) and were fairly evenly distributed throughout that range.

Table 3-1 summarizes the amounts of indirect costs reported by the various respondents.

TABLE 3-1

Total Indirect Cost as a Percentage of Revenues

Amount	No. of Firms	%
Under 2%	22	20.0%
2.1%–5%	31	28.2%
5.1%–10%	16	14.6%
10.1%–20%	15	13.6%
Over 20%	26	23.6%
Total	110	100.0%

A number of factors contributing to the varying amounts of indirect costs emerge from further analysis of the questionnaire responses and the in-depth interviews. These factors are discussed below.

1. *Role of Corporate Headquarters.* Some companies operate their corporate offices under the holding company concept, especially when the primary profit centers are organized as separate legal entities (subsidiaries). Under the holding company concept, the corporate office is thinly staffed, and most planning and control responsibilities are borne by profit center management. Costs are incurred only as required for the corporation as an entity. Few, if any, services are provided for the segments of the company. For example, the staffs in the profit centers of many holding companies are almost identical in structure to the staff in the corporate headquarters. In such a situation, corporate indirect costs are understandably quite low.

On the other hand, many companies operate their corporate offices under the operating company concept. Here, the corporate office plays a major and active role in corporate planning and control as well as in corporate service functions. Services provided by corporate headquarters include services for the entire firm as an entity as well as services for the various profit centers. Consequently, corporate indirect costs make up a sizable proportion of total revenues.

2. *Number of Levels in the Profit Center Structure.* As was mentioned earlier, indirect costs similar to corporate administrative costs and service costs also exist at every level of managerial responsibility in a company with a hierarchy of segments. Some respondents pointed out during in-depth interviews that many support functions were performed by the primary profit

centers and their subdivisions because the corporate service staffs could not provide all necessary services to components at the lower levels of responsibility. Thus, as the number of levels in the profit center structure increases, indirect costs spread out, and there is a corresponding decrease of the relative magnitude of corporate indirect costs. On the other hand, if the divisional structure of a company involves only one or two levels, more service functions may be centralized at the corporate level, and the relative amount of corporate indirect costs may increase accordingly.

3. *Centralized Versus Decentralized Operations.* If a company's operations are centralized, it is likely that its service functions are also centralized. In a decentralized organization, however, the service functions may be either provided centrally or performed by the individual operating segments. Hence, the amount of corporate indirect costs is likely to be larger in a centralized organization than in a decentralized firm. The survey results reported in Table 3-2 seem to bear this pattern out. With the exception of the banking industry, decentralized firms reported substantially smaller amounts of corporate indirect costs than centralized firms. As for the banking industry, the decentralization of profit centers does not appear to have any impact on the amount of corporate indirect costs. The questionnaire revealed that the banking industry

TABLE 3-2

Amount of Indirect Cost by Industries and Divisional Responsibility

(% of indirect cost to total revenues)

Industry	Centralized Firms*	Decentralized Firms*	All Firms
Banking	20.88%	20.33%	20.67%
Manufacturing	15.09%	8.11%	9.57%
Retail	13.56%	5.73%	10.95%
Service	14.00%	5.05%	9.18%
All others**	18.23%	7.13%	11.96%
Weighted average:			
All respondents	16.73%	8.58%	11.85%
All respondents except in banking	15.47%	7.36%	10.30%

* Differences between centralized firms and decentralized firms are significant at the 1% level.

** Industries with fewer than five respondents in either responsibility category are not listed separately.

has relatively high indirect costs. In-depth interviews with bankers suggested that most service activities are provided centrally in decentralized as well as centralized banks.

The findings reported here appear to be consistent with those of a recent research project on decentralization:

> The more diverse a firm, the more administrative services are performed at the profit center level. The less diverse Single and Dominant Business firms tend to centralize administrative costs because their profit centers usually contain only product management activities; administrative services such as financial analysis and accounting are centralized at the corporate level so as to serve all the profit centers in the firm.[2]

4. *Nature of the Industry.* Table 3-2 also summarizes the average amounts of corporate indirect costs in different industries. Banking clearly has the highest ratio of corporate indirect costs. The relative amounts of corporate indirect costs in other industries, however, do not appear to be significantly different.

Allocation of Corporate Indirect Costs Among Primary Profit Centers

Despite the overwhelming objections to indirect cost allocations found in the literature, most companies responding to this survey reported allocating corporate indirect costs among their primary profit centers. When asked whether they allocated any part of indirect costs among profit centers for any purpose, 84% (103 out of 123 respondents) said that they did and the remaining 16% said they did not.

The decision to allocate corporate indirect costs was clearly related to the number of primary profit centers reporting separate financial data in a company. Table 3-3 shows that the percentage of firms allocating corporate indirect costs is significantly higher among firms with six or more primary profit centers than in those with fewer than six. The reason for this difference probably can be explained by the theory of the span of control. One of the major reasons for allocating corporate indirect costs is to relate profit centers' earnings to total corporate profit (see Chapter 5 for further discussion). When the number of profit centers is small, the need to allocate indirect costs in order to reconcile corporate profit with the sum of profit centers' earnings may be avoided, because top management may be able to make the necessary adjustment mentally. As the number of primary profit centers grows, however, the need to allocate indirect costs becomes greater.

Classification of Corporate Costs as Direct or Indirect

In order for us to understand the nature of indirect costs better, survey

TABLE 3-3

Number of Firms Allocating Corporate Indirect Costs (Classified by the number of profit centers)

No. of Primary Profit Centers	Number of Firms Yes	No	Total	% Yes/Total*
1–5	11	7	18	61%
6–10	24	4	28	86%
11–20	23	4	27	85%
21–50	20	1	21	95%
51–100	5	1	6	83%
Over 100	19	1	20	95%
Over 5 subtotal	91	11	102	89%
Total	102	18	120	85%

* The difference between responses by firms with 1–5 profit centers and those with over 5 is significant at the 3% level.

respondents were asked to indicate whether each of 14 expenses normally found in corporate headquarters was (1) all direct costs, (2) all indirect costs, (3) part direct and part indirect, or (4) included in a general and administrative (G&A) expense pool. Table 3-4 summarizes the responses. Among these corporate expense items, only a few were considered all direct by more than a negligible number of respondents. Thus, in Table 3-4, responses classifying items either as all direct or as partially direct are combined in one set of totals in the first column. Those expenses classified as all direct and the percentages of respondents treating them as such are as follows:

Product marketing	41%
Research and development	30%
Corporate engineering and production	29%
Purchasing	19%
Interest on debt	16%

Interest on debt is really a special case. Approximately 70% of the banking respondents considered it all direct cost, while only 5% of all other respondents treated it so.

The fact that a single corporate expense item may be treated differently suggests that the line between direct and indirect costs is far from clear. The

TABLE 3-4

Classification of Corporate Expenses as Direct or Indirect by All Firms

Expenses	Percentage of Firms Considering the Expenses as: All Direct or Partially Direct	All Indirect	Included in G&A Pool
G&A Expenses	65%	35%	—
R&D*	72%	17%	11%
Personnel Functions	52%	27%	21%
Accounting	54%	22%	24%
Data Processing*	68%	20%	12%
Product Marketing*	66%	19%	15%
Corporate Engineering & Production	56%	29%	15%
Purchasing	55%	29%	16%
Public Relations & Corporate Promotion*	24%	48%	28%
Corporate Executives' Compensation	29%	40%	31%
Treasurer's Functions*	18%	53%	29%
Interest on Debt**	37%	50%	13%
Legal & Government Affairs	33%	41%	26%
Tax Department*	14%	54%	32%
Average	45%	35%	20%

* Significantly different from the average at the 1% level.

** With banks excluded, these percentages would be 30%, 55%, and 15%. These are significantly different from the average at the 2% level.

term "indirect costs" was defined in the survey questionnaire as "those costs incurred for the benefit of two or more components of a company in such a way that it is difficult to trace specific portions exclusively to individual components." Conversely, the term "direct costs" was defined as costs that are "wholly and exclusively traceable to a single component." Responses to the questionnaire and the in-depth interviews suggest that although traceability is a major factor in separating direct costs from indirect costs, a number of other factors may also contribute to the classification of corporate costs as direct or indirect. Apparently, traceability alone either is inadequate or is too vague a criterion for classifying costs as direct.

An analysis of questionnaire responses identified the following four additional factors that significantly affect the classification of corporate costs: (1) the nature of the cost item, (2) the size of the firm, (3) a policy of centralization or decentralization, and, to a lesser degree, (4) the nature of the industry.

Nature of the Cost Item

Two distinct types of corporate functions can be observed in Table 3-4—functions that may be performed at the division level as well as at the corporate level and functions that typically are performed only at the corporate level. The former include research and development, the personnel function, accounting, data processing, product marketing, corporate engineering and production, purchasing, and general and administrative functions. The majority of the survey respondents considered the costs of performing these functions at least partially direct to profit centers. This practice reflects a belief that part of these costs can be traced to activities at the divisional level, despite the difficulty of identifying a specific direct relationship between individual corporate costs and divisional activities. Among these corporate expenses, the tendencies to classify research and development, data processing, and product marketing as direct costs of profit centers are statistically significant.

On the other hand, public relations and corporate promotion, corporate executives' compensation, the treasurer's functions, interest on debt (except in banks, as noted earlier), legal and government affairs, and the tax department were most often considered all indirect costs by respondents. These are the types of functions that are required primarily by the corporation as an entity. The tendency to classify the costs of these functions as all indirect was statistically significant in the cases of public relations and corporate promotion, the treasurer's functions, and the tax department.

Size of the Firm

Table 3-5 compares the classifications of corporate costs by small firms and by medium and large firms. For purposes of this comparison, small firms are defined as those with annual sales of less than $100 million. The percentages of medium and large firms considering corporate costs as all or partially direct are greater than those of small firms, while the percentages of small firms treating corporate costs as all indirect are higher than those of medium and large firms. This difference is found consistently in all cases and is statistically significant at the 1% level. The percentages of firms treating individual corporate expenses as part of a general and administrative expense pool are almost identical in the two size groups.

Why larger firms are more likely to treat corporate costs as direct and smaller firms are more likely to treat them as indirect remains to be explained.

TABLE 3-5

Classification of Corporate Expenses as Direct or Indirect by Sizes of Firms

Expenses	Small Firms			Medium and Large Firms		
	All Direct or Partially Direct	All Indirect	Included in G&A	All Direct or Partially Direct	All Indirect	Included in G&A
G&A Expenses	31%	69%	—	72%	28%	—
R&D	25%	50%	25%	73%	16%	11%
Personnel Functions	28%	55%	17%	57%	22%	21%
Accounting	28%	50%	22%	59%	17%	24%
Data Processing	61%	33%	6%	69%	19%	12%
Product Marketing	44%	39%	17%	72%	14%	14%
Corporate Engineering & Production	50%	33%	17%	58%	29%	13%
Purchasing	41%	35%	24%	58%	28%	14%
Public Relations & Corporate Promotion	20%	60%	20%	25%	56%	29%
Corporate Executives' Compensation	17%	50%	33%	31%	39%	30%
Treasurer's Functions	11%	67%	22%	19%	51%	30%
Interest on Debt	33%	60%	7%	38%	48%	14%
Legal & Government Affairs	22%	56%	22%	34%	40%	26%
Tax Department	7%	60%	33%	15%	54%	31%
Average*	29%	52%	19%	48%	32%	20%

* The difference between small firms' classification and larger firms' classification is significant at the 1% level.

One can only speculate that, as a firm grows larger, its corporate service staffs also grow and become more specialized; hence, their costs become more readily traceable to individual segments of the firm.

Centralization or Decentralization of Operations

Table 3-6 presents the classifications of corporate expenses by centralized and decentralized firms. A consistent pattern can be observed. Decentralized firms are more likely than centralized firms to consider corporate expenses as direct costs. The latter are more likely than the former to regard costs as all indirect. The difference again is highly significant statistically.

Two possible explanations for this difference suggest themselves. First, since the segments of a centralized firm are usually not as clearly separated as those of a decentralized firm, distinguishing direct costs from indirect costs may be neither as necessary nor as practicable. Second, a profit center manager's decision to use corporate services helps to identify the related costs as direct in that center. And profit center managers in a decentralized corporation naturally have more decision-making authority than those in a centralized firm. This factor is discussed further later in this section.

Nature of the Industry

To a lesser extent, the nature of the industry in which a firm operates also plays some role in the classification of corporate costs as direct or indirect. As mentioned earlier, most banks considered interest on debt as all direct, while most nonbank respondents considered it all indirect. Another corporate expense classified differently by firms in different industries is product marketing. Sixty percent of manufacturers and conglomerates considered product marketing as all direct cost, while only 22% of the respondents in all other industries treated it as direct. This difference is statistically significant at the 1% level. It might be explained by the fact that manufacturing firms and conglomerates have more distinctive product lines and may be more likely to promote these products separately. The other industries in the survey (banking, insurance, retailing, transportation, and services) are less likely to promote individual product lines separately.

Other Factors

In addition to the foregoing four factors identified in an analysis of the questionnaires, two other factors affecting the classification of costs were reported by executives interviewed. These were (1) whose needs cause the corporate costs to be incurred and (2) whose decisions cause them to be incurred. These two factors seem to be operational interpretations of the causal relationship between division activities and corporate expenses. The move toward centralization of certain service functions for greater efficiency does not

TABLE 3-6

Classification of Corporate Expenses as Direct or Indirect by Centralized Firms and Decentralized Firms

	Centralized Firms			Decentralized Firms		
Expenses	All Direct or Partially Direct	All Indirect	Included in G&A	All Direct or Partially Direct	All Indirect	Included in G&A
G&A Expenses	49%	51%	—	75%	25%	—
R&D	53%	30%	17%	80%	12%	8%
Personnel Functions	38%	38%	24%	63%	18%	19%
Accounting	39%	37%	24%	65%	10%	25%
Data Processing	54%	34%	12%	78%	10%	12%
Product Marketing	52%	33%	15%	75%	9%	16%
Corporate Engineering & Production	52%	29%	19%	57%	30%	13%
Purchasing	35%	41%	24%	71%	18%	11%
Public Relations & Corporate Promotion	21%	51%	28%	25%	45%	30%
Corporate Executives' Compensation	32%	36%	32%	26%	43%	31%
Treasurer's Functions	14%	59%	27%	20%	49%	31%
Interest on Debt	30%	60%	10%	40%	44%	16%
Legal & Government Affairs	22%	49%	29%	40%	35%	25%
Tax Department	11%	54%	35%	13%	56%	31%
Average	35%*	43%*	22%	52%*	28%*	20%

* The difference between centralized firms and decentralized firms is significant at the 1% level.

change the fact that corporate services are provided mainly to meet the needs of divisions for those services. Thus, many respondents considered corporate service costs in reality to be direct costs of the divisions or profit centers.

Similarly, although service functions may be performed at the corporate level, the decision to use the services may be made by the profit center managers. Consequently, the costs of such services may reasonably be regarded as directly traceable to the profit centers, at least to the extent that the service costs vary with the volume of usage of the services. This use of decision-making authority as a basis for classifying costs as direct or indirect is consistent with the concept of responsibility accounting. An interesting example of this approach is one manufacturer's practice of classifying interest expense as a direct cost of operating divisions. Most manufacturers considered interest as an indirect cost. The executives of this company, however, felt that it should be considered direct because the use of capital is controlled at the division level, even though the financing is arranged at the corporate level.

It seems clear that traceability, although an obviously important factor, is not the only one considered in the classification of costs as direct. One might argue that the additional factors discussed above are not really independent factors but merely elements of the concept of traceability. This contention suggests that traceability is a broad and imprecise concept that requires further interpretation to make it operationally meaningful.

Extent of Indirect Cost Allocation

To help us gain further insight into the specifics of indirect cost allocation practices, respondents were asked to indicate the extent to which the 14 indirect cost items listed in the preceding section (see Table 3-4) were allocated to primary profit centers for each of the four purposes discussed in Chapter 2 (that is, performance evaluation, cost-based pricing, decision analysis, and financial reporting). Table 3-7 summarizes responses to the question of whether the *full* amount of each indirect cost, *part* of it, or *none* of it was allocated to primary profit centers for each purpose. There are two ways to view the data in Table 3-7. Vertically, one may compare the extent of allocation of each corporate expense with that of the others. Horizontally, one may see whether the same or different allocations of a single item are made for different purposes.

After the direct portion has been separated from the indirect portion of each corporate expense item, the indirect portion remaining is treated similarly by all respondents. The percentages of firms reporting full, partial, and no allocation of each indirect expense in each column are not statistically different among the 14 expense items. None of the demographic characteristics tested showed any difference in the extent of indirect cost allocation—with one exception. For performance evaluation, the percentage of small firms (sales less than $100 million) reporting full allocation of indirect costs is significantly

TABLE 3-7

Extent of Indirect Cost Allocation for Different Purposes

Expenses	Performance Evaluation			Cost-Based Pricing			Decision Analysis			Financial Reporting		
	Percentage of Firms Indicating the Extent of Allocation for Each Purpose											
	Full	Part	None	Full	Part	None	Full	Part	None	Full	Part	None
G&A Expenses	53%	31%	16%	48%	23%	29%	41%	23%	36%	45%	33%	26%
R&D	56	24	19	41	23	36	44	24	32	49	17	33
Personnel Functions	60	26	14	51	13	36	46	19	36	46	29	25
Accounting	59	24	17	47	15	38	41	20	39	48	29	23
Data Processing	62	27	12	57	13	29	50	22	28	51	23	26
Product Marketing	62	23	15	52	19	29	47	27	25	53	11	36
Corporate Engineering & Production	55	26	18	45	23	32	43	26	30	48	20	32
Purchasing	63	21	16	58	12	30	50	17	33	53	20	27
Public Relations & Corporate Promotion	54	19	26	45	11	44	42	14	44	45	18	37
Corporate Executives' Compensation	55	18	27	48	11	40	38	20	42	44	20	36
Treasurer's Functions	56	21	24	50	16	34	39	21	39	48	20	32
Interest on Debt	56	16	29	48	6	46	44	23	33	48	14	38
Legal & Government Affairs	56	25	19	48	16	37	40	20	40	49	22	29
Tax Department	57	19	24	48	13	39	41	16	43	49	21	30
Average	57%	23%	20%	49%	15%	36%	43%	21%	36%	48%	21%	31%
Average: Performance Evaluation vs. All Other Purposes Combined*	57%	23%	20%				47%	19%	34%			

* The difference is significant at the 2% level.

lower than that of medium and large firms. Only 39% of small firms, compared with 64% of medium and large firms, indicated full allocation. On the other hand, 32% of small firms, in contrast to 19% of medium and large firms, reported only partial allocation.

The survey respondents indicated higher percentages of indirect cost allocations for performance evaluation than for any other purpose. Comparing the percentages across the four sets of columns in Table 3-7, one finds no significant variation in the extent of allocation for cost-based pricing, decision analysis, and financial reporting. For performance evaluation, however, the extent of allocation is consistently higher than for the other three. This difference is statistically significant at the 2% level.

Periodic Review of Allocation Policies and Methods

Questionnaire respondents were asked to indicate how often they reviewed and, if necessary, revised their indirect cost allocation policies and methods. Their responses are summarized in Table 3-8. One can see that most companies review their allocation practices annually. A few companies reported that a review was undertaken at intervals even shorter than one year. What is examined in this periodic review and what changes may be made after it vary from company to company. Some firms' periodic reviews are really not examinations of policies and methods, since they are limited to redetermination of allocation rates. Other companies reported periodic debates between the corporate controller and profit center managers over both the philosophy of allocation and the specific expense items allocated.

It is interesting to note that some companies reported that their allocations of corporate indirect costs were accepted reluctantly by profit center management as a form of surcharge, much as income taxes are accepted reluctantly by most taxpayers. Other companies, however, reported that their division man-

TABLE 3-8
Frequency of Allocation Policy Review

Frequency of Review	Number of Firms	%
Annually	67	65%
Regularly at intervals longer than one year	10	10%
Only when required by major changes in operations or other conditions	26	25%

agers continued to challenge the practice of making indirect cost allocations at all. It remains to be determined what factors caused these differences in the degrees of acceptance of indirect cost allocations. A prevalent sentiment among the corporate executives interviewed was that, since independent companies must incur corporate expenses, operating divisions should be charged proportionate shares of indirect corporate costs so that comparisons with independent companies can be made.

Indirect Cost Allocation at Lower Levels

Every company visited for pilot testing of the questionnaire or for an in-depth interview indicated that its corporate controller had no control over how indirect costs are allocated at the lower levels of the organization. Although corporate allocation policies often served as guidelines for allocations at lower levels, significant differences appeared to exist for the following three reasons:

1. The breakdown of operations into smaller segments at the lower levels is often different from the divisionalization at the corporate level. The different organizational arrangements may require different allocation methods.
2. The nature of operations differs from one level to another. An executive of a large manufacturer observed that allocations of indirect costs at the corporate level were more pertinent to performance evaluation than to cost-based pricing or to decision analysis. In a company with a hierarchy of segments at various levels of management responsibility, pricing and other decisions are usually made at the lower levels. This difference in emphasis at different levels of responsibility might account for the greater extent of indirect cost allocation for performance evaluation than for the other three purposes, as reported earlier (see Table 3-7).
3. The degree of control that a manager at one level in the hierarchy has over indirect costs is likely to be significantly different from that of a manager at a higher or lower level.

Separation of Variable and Fixed Indirect Costs

The questionnaire also asked whether companies allocated variable and fixed indirect costs separately for each of the four purposes discussed in the study. Table 3-9 shows the responses. Obviously, most companies did not allocate variable and fixed costs separately. As will be discussed later (see Chapter 6), this omission may significantly limit the validity and the usefulness of allocations.

TABLE 3-9

Separate Allocations of Variable and Fixed Indirect Costs

Purposes	Yes	%	No	%
Performance Evaluation	28	29%	68	71%
Cost-Based Pricing	25	28%	65	72%
Decision Analysis	25	27%	69	73%
Financial Reporting	22	24%	70	76%

Use of Actual Costs Versus Predetermined Costs in Allocations

The final substantive question in the questionnaire asked whether the amounts of indirect costs allocated to primary profit centers were actual or predetermined amounts. Respondents who reported allocating predetermined amounts were then asked whether variances from actual amounts were allocated in the same proportions or were left unallocated. Replies are summarized in Table 3-10. Approximately equal numbers of firms reported using each of the two alternatives, with a few firms indicating the use of both. Differences in practices for the four purposes were not statistically significant. When predetermined amounts were allocated, variances from actual costs were not allocated in most cases. A common practice is to include variances in a pool of unabsorbed corporate expense, not charged to profit centers. If variances are allocated in the same proportions as the predetermined amounts, the net effect is the same as if actual costs were allocated.

TABLE 3-10

Allocation of Actual or Predetermined Indirect Costs

	Amount Allocated			If Predetermined, Variances Are	
Purposes	Actual Amount	Predetermined	Some of Each	Allocated	Unallocated
Performance Evaluation	41	40	9	9	31
Cost-Based Pricing	33	29	7	5	24
Decision Analysis	36	31	5	6	25
Financial Reporting	39	26	8	9	17

Summary

This chapter reports the results of a questionnaire survey and follow-up interviews regarding the allocation of corporate indirect costs. The respondents clearly distinguished two types of corporate costs: corporate administrative costs and corporate service costs. This distinction seems to have a strong influence on the classification of corporate expenses as direct or indirect, as do the size of the firm, the nature of the industry, and the centralization or decentralization of operations.

The amount of corporate indirect costs varies significantly. Factors contributing to the varying sizes of these corporate costs include managerial philosophy regarding the role of the corporate office, the number of levels in the corporate hierarchy, the centralization or decentralization of operations, and the nature of the industry.

Despite theoretical criticisms of indirect cost allocation, most companies responding to the survey reported allocating corporate indirect costs among their primary profit centers. Allocations of corporate indirect costs are made more frequently for purposes of performance evaluation than for cost-based pricing, decision analysis, or financial reporting.

Practices with respect to periodic review of allocation policies, separate allocation of variable and fixed costs, and the use of actual or predetermined allocation rates were also described in this chapter. Two major questions remain: On what bases are allocations made, and why are they made? These issues are discussed in the next two chapters.

Notes

1. George J. Staubus, *Activity Costing and Input–Output Accounting* (Homewood, Ill.: Richard D. Irwin, Inc., 1971), pages 142–143.

2. Richard F. Vancil, *Decentralization: Managerial Ambiguity by Design* (Homewood, Ill.: Dow Jones–Irwin, 1979), page 232.

Chapter 4

Allocation Bases

The preceding chapter reported various general practices concerning the classification and allocation of corporate indirect costs. This chapter addresses allocation methods. The primary methodological issue in an indirect cost allocation scheme is the choice of the allocation bases to be used for the various indirect cost pools. The selection of the cost pools themselves is also an issue, but it is usually resolved fairly readily by establishing pools along lines of responsibility centers or functions.

Once a firm decides that particular indirect costs will be allocated to primary profit centers, the choice of allocation bases determines how much of each cost will be allocated to each profit center. That, of course, is an issue of great concern to both corporate management and profit center managers. This chapter looks first at the criteria used by survey respondents in selecting allocation bases and then at the nature of the various bases actually used.

Criteria for Selecting Allocation Bases

Six criteria for choosing an allocation base were discussed in Chapter 2. They were (1) fairness or equity, (2) benefit, (3) cause, (4) independence of the cost objectives, (5) ability to bear the costs, and (6) neutrality. The first five of these criteria were addressed in the survey of corporate practices. After preliminary discussions and further consideration, it was decided that the criterion of neutrality should not be included in the questionnaire. To begin with, neutrality is a criterion that is applicable to only one purpose for allocations—decision analysis. Neutrality is that characteristic of an allocation that avoids generating information that might mislead the decision maker. Thus, what constitutes a neutral allocation depends upon the particular decision in question.

Since it is impossible to anticipate every decision that will have to be made, neutrality would not be a practical criterion for a regular system of allocation. Rather, neutral allocations would have to be tailor-made for each decision situation. Furthermore, neutrality is a relatively unfamiliar notion in the context of cost allocations and might easily have been confused with fairness by respondents.

Questionnaire respondents who do allocate at least some indirect costs were asked to indicate which of the five remaining criteria they actually used in deciding how to allocate. Their responses are summarized in Table 4-1. Since respondents were instructed to check as many of the criteria as they actually used, the responses add up to far more than 100%. The criteria were stated exactly as they appear in this table and were listed in the order shown there. Fairness was deliberately placed last in the list to minimize the possibility that respondents might see it first and identify it as the only criterion, without carefully considering the others. As is indicated in Table 4-1, fairness was chosen by a majority of the respondents; but it was not the most frequently mentioned criterion. Causal factors and benefits received were the most popular criteria.

TABLE 4-1

Criteria Used in Choosing Allocation Bases

	Number of Respondents	Percentage of Respondents
Benefits received by profit centers from indirect costs	75	73%
Factors that *cause* the indirect costs to be incurred	81	79%
A profit center's *ability to bear* the charge for indirect costs	17	17%
A principle that the amount allocated to one profit center should not be affected by actions or conditions in any other profit center	17	17%
Equity or *fairness* to all the parties involved	68	66%
Other criteria	10	10%

These choices are consistent with the dominant recommendations in the management accounting literature and also with the respondents' views of the nature of corporate indirect costs. It was noted in Chapter 3 that respondents clearly distinguished two types of indirect costs: corporate administrative costs and corporate service costs. The former were allocated to the primary profit centers mainly because corporate executives felt that these profit centers receive *benefits* from these costs. The latter were allocated to the primary profit centers principally because executives felt that the service costs were really *caused* by the profit centers. Therefore, it is not surprising that causal and beneficial factors were the most frequently cited criteria.

The notions of cause and benefit reflected in the questionnaire responses seem to be somewhat vague, however. Most respondents who indicated using cause as a criterion also reported using benefit. It is true that a causal relationship implies a certain beneficial relationship as well, but the reverse is not necessarily true. As mentioned in the preceding chapter, a causal relationship lends itself to fairly objective measurement, albeit with some element of arbitrariness. A purely beneficial relationship, on the other hand, cannot be measured with any degree of objectivity. These vague notions of cause and benefit are also reflected in the selection of allocation bases, to be considered later in this chapter.

The third criterion listed in Table 4-1, ability to bear, was surprisingly low in popularity. However, although only 17% of the respondents reported using it as a criterion for choosing allocation bases, a far greater percentage of the allocation bases actually used by respondents clearly reflect ability to bear.

The fourth criterion listed in Table 4-1 is, of course, the independence criterion. It was felt that this lengthier description of the criterion was necessary in order to avoid possible confusion. The notion of independence is not as familiar as the others listed, and it might have been interpreted as meaning simply that the profit centers operated independently of one another.

Ten respondents indicated that they used other criteria in selecting allocation bases. Seven of these actually specified the allocation bases that they used, however, not the logical basis on which they were chosen. Two firms mentioned the requirements of Cost Accounting Standard 403, "Allocation of Home Office Expenses to Segments." This, of course, is a compelling criterion for defense contractors subject to the Standard. Finally, one firm indicated that one of its criteria for choosing an allocation base was to obtain a more accurate assessment of profitability. This reason is really a justification for making allocations rather than a criterion for choosing a particular base. It does not suggest how one allocation base might result in a more accurate measurement of divisional profit than another.

Allocation Bases Actually Used

As might be expected, there was a greater diversity of responses to the question regarding the allocation bases used for various purposes and for different expense categories than to any other question asked. To report each and every allocation base used for each expense item would be both tiresome and pointless. Thus, the discussion that follows will focus on those allocation bases that were used most extensively. In this context, the extent of use of an allocation base has two dimensions. First, some companies reported using a single allocation base for all expense items and for all purposes or, at least, for all expense items for a single purpose. Second, certain allocation bases (for example, sales, net assets, and estimated time or usage) were reported by many companies for many different expense categories.

Thirty companies reported that they used a single allocation base for all expense categories (a maximum of 14) and for all four purposes. The allocation bases used by these companies are detailed in Table 4-2. Twenty-one of these firms used allocation bases that are very broad measures of operating activity or size (sales, net assets, total direct expenses, and unit volume). This is not surprising. If a single allocation base is to be used for many different expenses and for all purposes, one would expect it to be a broad one. A narrowly discriminating allocation base would hardly be suited to such a wide range of expense items. Six respondents used some formula combining two or more measures. These also suggest a broad allocation base. Note that the last allocation base listed in Table 4-2 is not really a base at all but, rather, one of the criteria for selecting an allocation base.

TABLE 4-2

Allocation Bases Used for All Expenses and All Purposes

	Number of Respondents
Sales or other operating revenue	8
Net assets	7
Total direct expenses	5
Unspecified formula	3
Equal weighting of sales, conversion costs, and assets	1
Equal weighting of sales, assets, and estimated services	1
Equal weighting of sales and investment	1
Unit volume	1
Estimated time, based on time analysis	1
Time and direct expenses	1
Ability to bear	1
	30

A few companies reported using a single allocation base for all expense categories for a single purpose. These responses are summarized in Table 4-3. Once again, the allocation bases used tend to be fairly broad ones. The principal difference between these data and those in Table 4-2 is the frequency with which employment data appear. These include the number of employees, employment expenses, and direct labor hours.

In many cases, a single allocation base was used for one expense category for all four purposes. At least four different bases were reported for each expense category. A complete listing of these responses would be of little

TABLE 4-3

Allocation Bases Used for All Expenses and One Purpose

	Number of Respondents
For purposes of performance evaluation:	
Net assets employed	2
Number of employees	1
Employment expenses	1
Estimated time	1
	5
For purposes of cost-based pricing:	
Sales or operating revenue	2
Employees and hours worked	1
	3
For purposes of decision analysis:	
Sales or operating revenue	2
Net capital employed	1
Employment expenses	1
	4
For purposes of financial reporting:	
Estimated time	1
Employment expenses	1
Average of sales, earnings, and capital	1
	3

value. Thus, the list of allocation bases by expense classes in Table 4-4 is limited to those bases or types of bases that were mentioned four or more times. For this purpose, such bases as the number of employees, head count, and payroll are combined together under the designation "employment data." Similarly, any allocation base that included two or more different measures is reported here simply as a "formula combining various factors," except in one case (data processing) in which a unique combination was reported by eleven respondents.

TABLE 4-4

Allocation Bases Used for One Expense and All Purposes

	Number of Respondents
G&A expenses:	
Formula combining various factors	17
Sales	11
Employment data	6
Total expenses before allocations	5
Research and development:	
Estimated time or usage	9
Formula combining various factors	4
Personnel functions:	
Employment data	29
Formula combining various factors	5
Accounting:	
Estimated time or usage	15
Sales	7
Employment data	5
Formula combining various factors	4
Data processing:	
All data processing resources used	18
Weighting of man and machine hours	11
CPU time	5
Standard hours	4
Sales	4

Product marketing:	
Formula combining various factors	10
Sales	8
Estimated time or usage	4
Public relations and corporate promotion:	
Formula combining various factors	9
Sales	8
Total expenses before allocation	4
Corporate engineering and production:	
Estimated time or usage	7
Direct costs	4
Purchasing:	
Dollar value of purchase orders	8
Number of purchase orders	6
Sales	6
Estimated time or usage	5
Formula combining various factors	5
Employment data	4
Corporate executives' salaries:	
Sales	8
Formula combining various factors	8
Estimated time or usage	5
Treasurer's functions:	
Sales	7
Estimated time or usage	7
Formula combining various factors	6
Interest on debt:	
Total capital employed	22
Legal and government affairs:	
Estimated time or usage	15
Formula combining various factors	9
Sales	8
Tax department:	
Estimated time or usage	10
Sales	8

Many of the allocation bases in Table 4-4 clearly reflect the criteria of cause (for example, CPU time for data processing and estimated time or usage for accounting) and benefit (for example, employment data for personnel functions). Others seem to suggest the ability-to-bear criterion (for example, sales and employment data for G&A expenses). The frequent use of estimated time or usage of services suggests that many companies make an effort to analyze certain indirect costs almost as though they were traceable direct costs. Estimated time or usage is probably reasonably accurate for such identifiable corporate services as research and development and accounting. One must wonder, however, how accurate estimates of corporate executives' time can be.

Comparisons of the criteria used by individual firms in selecting allocation bases with the allocation bases actually used by those firms did not reveal any consistent patterns. Quite different allocation bases were chosen by different firms that alleged to use common criteria. Conversely, differing criteria often led different firms to the same allocation base. This lack of a pattern is consistent with the notion that any allocation of truly indirect costs is inevitably arbitrary. An allocation base that suggests cause or benefit to one person may not to another, for example.

An interesting insight into the relationship between criteria and allocation bases was obtained in the in-depth interview with one respondent. The firm had indicated in its questionnaire that benefit and cause were its two selection criteria. However, net investment in assets was the sole allocation base used for all expense categories and all purposes. In general, net assets is an allocation base that reflects the ability-to-bear criterion. This particular respondent explained that the benefit in its case was to total corporate profit and that this was caused by profit center managers' control of their investments in assets. The firm operated in an industry characterized by low profit margins. Hence, a satisfactory return on investment depended upon a rapid turnover of the investment in assets. Thus, profit center managers were being motivated to keep their asset balances as low as possible by charging them for general corporate costs in proportion to their asset holdings. Although this procedure would not necessarily reduce all corporate indirect costs, it would tend to reduce interest expense. This particular use of net investment in assets as the only allocation base is consistent with the behavioral objective of the indirect cost allocation, but it does not reflect a true causal or beneficial relationship.

Summary

This chapter has discussed the criteria used by survey respondents in selecting allocation bases and the nature of the various bases actually used. A major observation was that the bases selected do not seem to reflect the criteria that the respondents said they used to select those bases. Few respondents mentioned ability to bear as the criterion that they used to select bases, but it appeared to be the dominant factor underlying the actual bases employed. A large number of respondents, however, did use bases reflecting causal factors to allocate those corporate service costs that are caused mainly by division operations.

Chapter 5

Reasons for Allocating and Not Allocating Indirect Costs

The preceding two chapters have described the actual practices of business firms with respect to indirect cost allocations for four specific purposes. This chapter addresses the reasons firms do and do not allocate indirect costs for those four purposes. It was reported in Chapter 3 that, despite theoretical objections, allocation of corporate indirect costs was quite widespread. An analysis of the reasons for allocations will shed some light on this finding. No additional insight is gained regarding the selection of allocation bases, however.

Reasons are inevitably more elusive and imprecise than practices, of course. Different firms may adopt similar practices for quite different reasons or combinations of reasons. Firms may also recognize reasons both for and against a particular practice. Thus, the final choice reflects a compromise between conflicting objectives. Moreover, the reasons for certain practices that have been followed consistently for many years may be lost in the mists of time. In the in-depth interview with one respondent, the individual acknowledged that he could not explain the reason for a particular practice, which appeared to be inconsistent with the firm's basic philosophy regarding cost allocations. The practice had been in use for many years, and no one had raised any significant objections to it. Yet, at one time, that practice had been selected from among potential alternatives for some reason.

The reasons for making or not making indirect cost allocations that were provided in the questionnaire were reasons advanced in the cost allocation literature. Respondents could add other reasons for allocating or not allocating indirect costs for each purpose. They were then asked to indicate as many reasons as they considered applicable in each case and to rank them in order of importance when more than one reason was given. The following sections summarize the responses. Both the frequency with which each reason was cited and the average ranking of each are reported.

Statistical Method Used in Analysis of Rankings

The statistical technique used in this chapter to analyze the potential differences in the rankings of various reasons by different groups of respondents is Kendall's rank correlation coefficient of concordance (W).[1] The coefficient of concordance is a measure of the degree of agreement among different judges' rankings of a set of object items (reasons, in this instance). The object items to be ranked have no known intrinsic order established by any criterion. Two or more judges rank the object items with respect to some attribute (importance in this case), and the coefficient of concordance is a measure of the degree of agreement among the judges. This coefficient reflects the similarity of opinions and value judgments of different judges.

A high value of W indicates that different groups of respondents are applying essentially the same standards or frames of reference to the reasons being ranked. If the coefficient of concordance is significant at the 1% level, it means that there is only one chance in a hundred that agreement on rankings by different groups of respondents was a random occurrence or coincidence, attributable merely to chance. Conversely, there are 99 chances in 100 that the agreement reflects a significant and systematic consistency in points of view among the various respondents.

One basic assumption of the coefficient of concordance is an equal interval between ranks. For example, if three object items, A, B, and C, have average rankings of 1.2, 1.8, and 2.1, respectively, the rank order for A, B, and C for statistical test purposes will be 1, 2, and 3, respectively.

If a particular item was ranked by only one or two respondents in a demographic group, the average ranking of that particular item may not be as meaningful as the average rankings of those cited more frequently. In order to avoid the distortion of a ranking by one or two extreme cases, those items ranked by fewer than three respondents in a demographic group were excluded from the statistical test of the ranking. All items so eliminated in this study had negligible frequencies and were ranked relatively low by respondents.

The coefficient of concordance is highly significant for all cases except one in this study. Thus, the reasons for allocating or not allocating indirect corporate costs are essentially the same among all respondents. For this reason, only the summary data are reported in this chapter, except in the one case in which the coefficient of concordance was not significant. The reasons for allocating or not allocating indirect costs are listed in the tables in this chapter in the order of their average rankings. The order in which they appeared in the questionnaire may be found in Appendix B.

Allocations for Financial Reporting

Indirect cost allocations for purposes of external financial reporting were not a major objective of this study. Questions regarding practices in this area were included principally to provide a point of reference for reviewing allocation practices for internal management purposes. As was seen in Chapter 3, there are some significant differences in the extent of allocations for these different purposes.

One hundred and one respondents answered a question about their firms' positions with regard to allocation of indirect costs to "reportable segments" in accordance with the requirements of the Financial Accounting Standards Board[2] or similar requirements of government regulatory agencies. Their responses are summarized in Table 5-1. The statements in this table represent reasons for allocating or not allocating corporate indirect costs among segments in external financial statements. Obviously, most of the respondents' practices in this respect are directly consistent with authoritative pronouncements. That is, most firms either allocate in accordance with the standards or regulations or do not allocate if not required to do so.

TABLE 5-1

Attitudes Toward Allocations for Segment Reporting in External Financial Statements

	Frequency
We report segment profit data in accordance with requirements and believe that such reporting is appropriate and useful.	44
We report segment profit data and allocate indirect costs only because of requirements but we believe that such data are not useful to investors and other outside users of financial statements.	13
We report segment profit data and allocate indirect costs to segments even though we are not required to do so.	8
We are not required to report segment profit data and do not do so.	36

It is interesting to note that, of the 57 firms that were required to allocate, 77% agreed that the resulting segment profit data are appropriate and useful. Only 23% disagreed with the requirement. (One respondent indicated in an in-depth interview that he believes that the specific FASB requirement is not useful but that the allocation of indirect costs would be useful if it reflected each industry's peculiar situation.) Of the 44 firms not required to report segment profit data, only 18% elected to do so voluntarily.

Forty-nine of the 65 respondents that indicated they do allocate indirect costs for segment reporting purposes replied to a question regarding the reason for the extent to which allocations were made. Seventy-one percent of these respondents stated that they considered their allocation practices to be exactly in accordance with the requirements of the Financial Accounting Standards Board. The remaining 29% indicated that they allocate more than the minimum amount of indirect costs required by the standard because they believe that the resulting profit data provide a better depiction of their firms' profitabilities.

Allocations for Performance Evaluation

As noted in Chapter 3, more firms reported allocating indirect costs for internal performance evaluation than for any of the other purposes addressed in this study. Their reasons for making allocations for this particular purpose are presented in Table 5-2. Most respondents gave more than one reason for allocating. A total of 91 respondents to this question chose a total of 266 reasons, or an average of almost three reasons per respondent.

Respondents who selected more than one reason were asked also to rank these reasons in the order of their importance. A few did not provide this ranking, despite their choosing more than one reason. In these cases, all reasons cited were interpreted as being considered of equal importance. The reasons for allocating included in Table 5-2 are listed in the order of their average ranking by all 91 respondents. Thus, it is possible for a single reason to be mentioned by more respondents than another but not to be considered as important as that other. This distinction may be seen in connection with the second and third reasons listed in Table 5-2.

The percentages in Table 5-2, as well as those in Tables 5-4 through 5-8, are percentages of the number of firms that provided reasons listed in that particular table (91 in the case of Table 5-2), not of the total number of respondents to the survey. In general, each respondent provided reasons either for allocating or for not allocating indirect costs for each different purpose. Thus, each respondent would be represented in either Table 5-2 or Table 5-4 (but not in both), in Table 5-5 or Table 5-6, and in Table 5-7 or Table 5-8. As a matter of fact, a few firms did provide reasons both for allocating and for not allocating for one purpose because they allocated certain indirect costs but not others.

In addition to the average rankings by all respondents, rankings of reasons for allocating were analyzed by various categories of respondents. These categories are as follows: industry classifications (categories shown in Table A-1 in Appendix A), sizes of firms (small, medium, or large), management philosophies regarding centralization or decentralization, the number of primary profit centers (categories shown in Table 3-3), and the magnitude of indirect costs as a percentage of revenue (categories shown in Table 3-1).

TABLE 5-2

Reasons for Allocating Indirect Costs for Purposes of Performance Evaluation

	Average Rank	Frequency of Mention No.	%
Reasons Provided in Questionnaire			
To remind profit center managers that indirect costs exist and that profit center earnings must be adequate to cover some share of those costs.	1.48	82	90%
To relate profit center earnings to total company profit so that the sum of all centers' profits is equal to company profit.	1.94	52	57%
Because the allocation methods used fairly reflect each profit center's usage of essential common services.	2.12	59	65%
To stimulate profit center managers to put pressure on central managers to control service costs.	2.33	42	46%
To encourage use of central services that would otherwise be underutilized.	3.05	21	23%
To minimize state or local taxes.	3.14	7	8%
Reasons Added by Respondents			
To determine divisional contribution to corporate overhead and profit better.	*	1	1%
To provide a true reflection of the cost of operation of each division.	*	1	1%
To ensure a minimum level of profitability at each profit center that visibly maintains corporate overhead.	*	1	1%

* An average rank is not meaningful when a reason is given by only one respondent.

Kendall's coefficient of concordance was calculated to determine the degree of agreement or disagreement in rankings of reasons among the respondents in these five categories. Those in four of the five categories showed a very high degree of agreement. The coefficient of concordance was significant at the 1% level in each of these four categories. The one exception was in the size category. Firms classified as small, medium, and large showed significantly different rankings from one another. No reason for this one area of disagreement on rankings is apparent.

In particular, size did *not* make any difference in rankings of reasons for allocating for the other purposes covered in the study (see tables 5-3 and 5-7). The rankings of the first four reasons listed in Table 5-2 by small, medium, and large firms are shown in Table 5-3. The coefficient of concordance was calculated for only these four reasons because fewer than three respondents in one or more categories selected each of the remaining reasons given in Table 5-2.

TABLE 5-3

Rankings of Reasons for Allocating for Performance Evaluation by Size of Respondents

	Ranking by		
	Small Firms	Medium Firms	Large Firms
To remind profit center managers that indirect costs exist and that profit center earnings must be adequate to cover some share of those costs.	2	2	1
To relate profit center earnings to total company profit so that the sum of all centers' profits is equal to company profit.	1	3.5*	2
Because the allocation methods used fairly reflect each profit center's usage of essential common services.	3	1	3
To stimulate profit center managers to put pressure on central managers to control service costs.	4	3.5*	4

* Indicates tie for third and fourth rank.

In Table 5-2, it is apparent that the single most important reason for allocating indirect costs for performance evaluation is "to remind profit center managers that indirect costs exist and that profit center earnings must be adequate to cover some share of those costs." This reason was cited by 90% of the respondents who allocate indirect costs for performance evaluation. This finding sheds some light on the allocation practices reported in Chapters 3 and 4.

First, the popularity of this reason may explain why the extent of allocation for performance evaluation is greater than for the other three purposes. By comparing Table 5-2 with Tables 5-5 and 5-7, one will notice that no other reason for indirect cost allocation for any purpose was cited by more than 60 respondents. Thus, it seems reasonable that more companies allocated corporate indirect costs for performance evaluation than for any other purpose mainly because of this one reason.

Second, "to remind profit center managers that indirect costs exist" is essentially a behavioral objective. That is, it implies that corporate management's principal reason for allocating costs to profit centers is to influence those centers' managers to conduct their operations in ways that will tend to produce satisfactory corporate profits. Consequently, the exact amount of the allocation is less important than the fact that the allocation is made at all. If profit center managers accept the notion that they have some share of corporate indirect costs to bear, the fact that the "correct" amount of that share cannot be determined need not deter the assignment of *some* share. Furthermore, the selection of an allocation base is less critical if one adopts this view of the purpose of the allocation. This fact may help explain the observation in Chapter 4 that most allocation bases used in practice seemed to reflect a broad, ability-to-bear criterion rather than a more refined measure of cause.

In the in-depth interviews with selected questionnaire respondents, the effect of allocations in performance reports on managers' compensation was investigated. Eight of these interviewees stated that segment profits computed after deducting allocations of indirect costs were used, either directly or indirectly, in determining segment managers' compensation. In five of these eight firms, only predetermined amounts of indirect costs were allocated to the profit centers. Thus, the allocations really made no difference in the amounts of the reported profits on which compensation was based, at least partly. In the other three firms, actual corporate costs were allocated to primary profit centers. In each of these three cases, the interviewee mentioned either that complaints about allocations had been received from profit center managers or that a system for appealing the amounts allocated had been established.

Thirty-three companies provided a total of 72 reasons they did *not* allocate indirect costs for purposes of performance evaluation. These reasons are summarized in Table 5-4. As in Table 5-2, the reasons are listed in the order of their importance, as reflected in the average rankings by all respondents. No statistics on comparative rankings by firms in different categories are provided here, however, because the number of firms in each category that cited each reason was too small to permit a meaningful calculation of the average ranking and the resultant coefficient of concordance.

Allocations for Cost-Based Pricing

Sixty-six companies offered a total of 167 reasons for allocating indirect corporate costs for purposes of cost-based pricing. These reasons are detailed

TABLE 5-4

Reasons for Not Allocating Indirect Costs for Purposes of Performance Evaluation

	Average Rank	Frequency of Mention No.	Frequency of Mention %
Reasons Provided in Questionnaire			
Because indirect costs are not related to individual profit centers and, thus, allocations are arbitrary and tend to distort reported center profits.	1.27	26	79%
Because profit center managers object to charges for costs that they cannot control.	1.86	22	67%
Because indirect costs are relatively immaterial in amount and would not significantly affect reported center profits.	2.38	8	24%
Because profit center managers cannot agree on a method of allocation.	2.60	6	18%
Because the clerical costs of making the allocations would be greater than any possible benefits.	3.00	9	27%
Reasons Added by Respondents			
Cost allocation has low priority relative to other system developments.	*	1	3%

* Average rank is not meaningful.

in Table 5-5. Once again, companies in all categories (industry, size, centralized or decentralized, number of primary profit centers, and magnitude of indirect costs in relation to revenues) agreed on their rankings of these reasons. Kendall's coefficient of concordance was significant at the 4% level, at least, in all categories.

Forty-two respondents provided a total of 77 reasons for *not* allocating indirect costs among primary profit centers for purposes of cost-based pricing. These reasons are listed in Table 5-6. The first reason listed there is really an

TABLE 5-5

Reasons for Allocating Indirect Costs for Purposes of Cost-Based Pricing

	Average Rank	Frequency of Mention No.	Frequency of Mention %
Reasons Provided in Questionnaire			
To recover a fair share of indirect costs in the price of each product line.	1.48	56	85%
To remind product line managers that indirect costs exist and must be covered by products' prices, even though prices are not based directly on costs.	1.78	50	76%
Because the allocation methods used fairly reflect each product's share of essential common costs and, thus, these shares should be included in prices.	1.85	40	61%
Because prices are set by government regulations and the allocation of indirect costs is required by those regulations.	1.89	19	29%
Reasons Added by Respondents			
An understanding of true costs is necessary for setting prices.	*	1	2%
Allocation of indirect costs enables us to unbundle pricing of services so that each service can be marketed independently.	*	1	2%

* Average rank is not meaningful.

argument that cost-based pricing is not relevant for the firms selecting it. The next three reasons in the list—and particularly the third and fourth—are all suggestive of a common theme, namely, a direct costing approach to cost-based pricing. A comparative analysis of the rankings of reasons for not allocating by firms in the five categories mentioned before could not be made because too few firms in each category chose each of the different reasons. Thus, Kendall's coefficient of concordance could not be computed reliably.

TABLE 5-6

Reasons for Not Allocating Indirect Costs for Purposes of Cost-Based Pricing

	Average Rank	Frequency of Mention No.	Frequency of Mention %
Reasons Provided in Questionnaire			
Because prices are determined by market forces beyond management's control. Cost allocations would not affect them.	1.39	28	67%
Because allocations are arbitrary and the resultant "full costs" are not reliable bases for pricing.	1.61	18	43%
Because product line managers are free to set their own prices and their profit margins are adequate to cover indirect costs as well as direct costs.	1.75	8	19%
Because our pricing policy is designed to provide a contribution margin from each product high enough so that all indirect costs are recovered.	2.05	20	48%
Reasons Added by Respondents			
Pricing is centralized for all divisions.	*	1	2%
Pricing policies are determined by changes in direct costs and market factors.	*	1	2%
We do not have the technical ability to allocate appropriately.	*	1	2%

* Average rank is not meaningful.

Allocations for Decision Analysis

Sixty-nine respondents offered a total of 124 reasons for allocating indirect costs to primary profit centers for purposes of decision analysis. These reasons are summarized in Table 5-7. The first reason in this listing was included in the questionnaire specifically to give respondents the opportunity to reject it. It is precisely the antithesis of the universally recognized fact that only incremental costs are relevant in decision analyses. Thus, indirect cost allocations, as such, are not relevant. It was surprising, therefore, to find that a large majority of the respondents who said they did allocate for purposes of decision analysis not only chose this theoretically invalid reason for doing so but also ranked it as the most important reason. Consequently, this particular response was pursued in the in-depth interviews with those firms that selected it.

In each case, the explanation for the response was essentially a denial of the fallacious argument inherent in it. One interviewee explained that only variable indirect costs were allocated for decision analysis. This explanation suggests that the costs involved, although accounted for as indirect, are actually direct costs that are traceable to specific decisions. The subjective nature of the indirect cost classification (noted in Chapter 3) is again evident. Costs may be accounted for as indirect simply because they are incurred at the corporate level, even though logically they may be traceable to activities at the other levels in the firm.

Another explanation was that the firm assumes that indirect costs will increase more or less in proportion to current allocation rates when decisions have the effect of increasing the volume of business. Actually, this reason is the second one listed in Table 5-7; indirect costs may be suitable surrogates for anticipated incremental indirect costs. One interviewee explained that he had interpreted the response to mean that *some* indirect costs are relevant to decision analysis and that his firm did not use allocations, as such, for this purpose.

Obviously, these interviewees constituted only a small minority of all respondents who chose that particular reason for allocating. Still, their explanations were all essentially the same: They did not really mean what the reason says. One can only speculate on the explanations that other respondents might offer. It is possible that the wording of that option was confusing, although it was recognized as being clear—and clearly wrong—in the preliminary field test of the questionnaire. It is interesting to note that none of the five additional reasons supplied by respondents really corresponds to the fallacious view that allocations, as such, are relevant for decision making. Rather, they all suggest a concern for recognition of the relevance of some amount of indirect costs.

Respondents in all five categories (industry, size, centralized or decentralized, number of primary profit centers, and magnitude of indirect costs) were in close agreement on their rankings of the reasons for allocating

TABLE 5-7

Reasons for Allocating Indirect Costs for Purposes of Decision Analysis

	Average Rank	Frequency of Mention No.	%
Reasons Provided in Questionnaire			
Because allocations of indirect costs are relevant to the determination of the effect of a proposed decision on company profit.	1.11	57	83%
Because current indirect cost allocation amounts are considered to be the best available approximations of expected actual increases in indirect cost categories.	1.82	34	49%
Because the proposed decision is expected to affect future allocations of indirect costs to profit centers. Thus, the allocation now is intended to inform profit center managers what future allocations are likely to be.	2.00	28	41%
Reasons Added by Respondents			
To review the overall profitability of business units at the corporate level.	*	1	1%
Assessment of a stand-alone competitive unit is required to assess broad competitive strength or weakness.	*	1	1%
To reflect each segment's share of support function costs in arriving at their profitability.	*	1	1%
Allocations are made if local management action increases indirect costs.	*	1	1%
To place all business units on a more equal basis when allocating scarce resources.	*	1	1%

* Average rank is not meaningful.

indirect costs for purposes of decision analysis. Kendall's coefficient of concordance was significant at the 1% level for all five categories of firms.

Table 5-8 details reasons given for *not* allocating for purposes of decision making. Forty-nine respondents provided a total of 68 reasons here. The two reasons given in the questionnaire are the familiar arguments against allocation found in the literature: Indirect costs are irrelevant if they will not be affected by the decision, and allocations are too arbitrary to provide useful information. The first reason added by one respondent would also be consistent with the general view if it had said that decisions are based on *contribution* margins only rather than on *gross* margins. Because of the small number of responses in individual categories, no statistical comparison of the rankings of responses by firms in the five categories could be made. It is interesting to note that, although the reasons for not allocating well reflect the general injunctions against it in the literature, more firms gave reasons they *do* allocate for decision analysis than gave reasons they *do not*.

TABLE 5-8

Reasons for Not Allocating Indirect Costs for Purposes of Decision Analysis

	Average Rank	Frequency of Mention No.	Frequency of Mention %
Reasons Provided in Questionnaire			
Because indirect costs, as such, are not expected to be affected by the decisions made and, hence, are irrelevant to the decision analysis.	1.05	39	80%
Because the arbitrary nature of allocations tends to create an artificial picture of profits expected to result from decisions.	1.52	27	55%
Reasons Added by Respondents			
Decisions are based on gross margins only.	*	1	2%
The impact of a decision on a division's costs is evaluated separately.	*	1	2%

* Average rank is not meaningful.

Summary

This chapter has discussed respondents' reasons for allocating or not allocating corporate indirect costs. For financial reporting purposes, indirect cost allocation practices were generally consistent with authoritative pronouncements, and most respondents agreed that the resulting segment profit data were appropriate and useful. For performance evaluation, the single most important reason for allocating indirect costs was to remind profit center managers that indirect costs exist and must be recovered through the earnings of the profit centers. This reason essentially is behavioral in nature. It implies that the major reason for indirect cost allocations may be to influence division managers' behavior rather than to measure "correct" division costs or profits. The dominant reasons given for allocating indirect costs for purposes of cost-based pricing were all variations on one theme—the desire to recover a fair share of all costs through the prices of all products. The principal reason given for indirect cost allocations for decision analysis was inconsistent with conventional wisdom. Interviews with several respondents suggested that the seemingly illogical reason simply may have reflected different interpretations of the concepts and terms in question.

Notes

1. M. G. Kendall, *Rank Correlation Methods*, 2nd edition (London: Charles Griffin & Company, Ltd., 1955).

2. *Financial Reporting for Segments of a Business Enterprise*, Statement of Financial Accounting Standards No. 14 (Stamford, Conn.: Financial Accounting Standards Board, 1976).

Chapter 6

Summary, Conclusions, and Recommendations

This chapter summarizes some of the principal findings of this study, presents critical comments regarding several of the findings, and offers recommendations for practical applications. It is not a complete, sequential summary of the entire research report, however. Such a summary appeared at the end of Chapter 1, and each subsequent chapter contained its own summary.

Cost Classifications

Distinguishing Between Direct and Indirect Costs

The accounting literature generally suggests that there is a fairly clear dichotomous classification of costs as direct or indirect with respect to any given cost objective. The cost objectives in question in this study are the primary profit centers of business corporations. Thus, the literature would suggest that direct costs are wholly traceable to individual profit centers, whereas indirect costs are common to two or more of the centers and are not even partially traceable to any single profit center. Consequently, costs may be charged to profit centers by either of two clearly distinct accounting procedures. That is, direct costs are charged in total to appropriate centers on the basis of unequivocal identifiable relationships. Indirect costs, on the other hand, can be allocated only among profit centers on some intuitively reasonable but ultimately arbitrary basis.

The survey reported here indicates that this distinction is not so clear as it may seem. Management judgment and certain arbitrary classifications enter into the accounting for many cost items. To begin with, there is a fairly general tendency to classify all costs incurred at the corporate level as indirect costs, even when substantial portions of such costs may be traceable quite directly to individual profit centers. In other words, costs tend to be classified as direct or indirect according to *where* they are incurred, regardless of *why* they are incurred. There are also some contrary tendencies. These are less predominant but clearly noticeable in the survey research.

Although traceability is the general criterion for classifying costs as direct, other factors also play significant roles. The nature of the cost item, for example, influences its classification. Costs of functions performed at the corporate level that could also be performed at the profit center level are likely to be considered at least partially direct. Examples of such functions are research and development, data processing, product marketing, and purchasing. Costs of other functions that almost inevitably must be performed at the corporate level are generally treated entirely as indirect costs. Examples of these types of functions are those of the treasurer, the tax department, the public relations department, and top corporate management. Other factors observed to play some significant role in the classification of certain costs as direct or indirect are the size of the corporation, its management philosophy with respect to centralization or decentralization, and, to a lesser extent, the industry in which it operates. Actually, banking was the only industry in which a marked tendency to classify very large proportions of costs as indirect was noted.

Two Different Types of Indirect Costs

One of the most significant findings of this study was a general tendency to distinguish between two types of indirect costs at the corporate level. These are identified here as corporate administrative costs and corporate service costs. Corporate administrative costs are those costs that must be incurred in any corporate entity and are necessarily incurred in the central corporate office. Examples include top executives' salaries, the treasurer's functions, and the operations of a tax department. Corporate service costs, on the other hand, are costs of services that typically are performed at the corporate level because it is more efficient to do so but that could also be performed separately in the individual profit centers. Data processing, accounting, and purchasing are examples of such services. Presumably, they are performed at the corporate level simply because it is less costly for the corporation as a whole than it would be to have them performed in each segment separately.

This distinction between corporate administrative costs and service costs is particularly useful in an evaluation of cost allocation practices. Allocations of corporate service costs are more likely to be defensible on causal grounds. Hence, they may be justified, to some extent at least, for purposes of evaluating performance in individual profit centers and for certain types of decision making. Profit center managers are more likely to be able to influence the total amount of corporate service costs by the volume of their demands for services, although they are not in a position to control the costs of the various inputs that go into the performance of the services. They probably can have no significant influence on corporate administrative costs, however. Furthermore, corporate service costs are more likely to have significant elements of variable costs in them. Thus, they can be influenced by decisions that will cause a change in the volume of operations. Corporate administrative costs, on the other hand, are typically fixed costs. They are less likely to change as operations change.

The distinction between corporate administrative and service costs should be recognized formally in the design of an accounting system. Not only does it suggest which costs should and should not be allocated, but it also suggests the type of allocation base that should be used for a particular cost category. In general, corporate service costs should be allocated on the basis of some causal factor. If demand from the profit centers really does affect the amount of these costs, the allocation base should reflect this fact.

Corporate administrative costs, on the other hand, if they are allocated at all, should be allocated on the basis of inferred benefits received by the profit centers or simply on the basis of the profit centers' abilities to bear the additional costs. For example, one might assume that a profit center benefits from the work of the corporate treasurer's office or from interest on borrowed capital in proportion to its share of the total capital employed by the firm. Alternatively, total capital employed might be used as the allocation base simply because it is a measure of the size of a profit center. Thus, each center is presumed to be able to bear a share of corporate administrative costs that is proportionate to its size.

Prevalence of Indirect Costs Allocation

Despite the almost universal theoretical injunctions against allocating indirect costs, most companies do allocate them, at least for some purposes. In fact, allocation of indirect costs is used most often for purposes of internal performance evaluation, yet this is a purpose for which the theoretical literature argues that allocations are particularly inappropriate. Clearly, managers perceive a need for allocations that dominates the conceptual difficulty of making them. The reasons for this compelling interest in allocation are discussed in the sections that follow. One consequence of the widespread use of allocations, despite the problems of making them, is a wide variety of practices, especially in the choice of allocation bases. No systematic patterns were observed in this study. It appears that allocation methods are selected because they are considered to be necessary, not because they appear to be uniquely appropriate in specific circumstances. This emphasis on allocations is particularly notable in firms with more than five primary profit centers, but a majority of firms with five or fewer profit centers also made allocations.

Selection of Allocation Bases

Probably the most significant procedural problem in allocating indirect costs is the choice of an allocation base. This survey sought to address two aspects of the allocation base selection problem. First, what criterion or criteria are used in selecting bases? Then, what bases are actually chosen? Factors that cause the indirect costs to be incurred and benefits received by profit centers were the most widely cited criteria. A profit center's ability to bear a particular share of indirect costs was mentioned by relatively few firms.

Still, the allocation bases that were actually used by these firms more often suggested ability to bear than cause or benefit. In particular, when a single allocation base was used for all cost items and all purposes, it was usually a very broad measure of activity (such as sales, net assets, or total direct costs). Such a broad measure suggests that the allocation base is simply the size of each profit center, and size is clearly an indication of ability to bear, not of cause or benefit. Cause and benefit should lead to more specific allocation bases, such as the number of employees as a base for allocating personnel costs and computer time as a base for allocating costs of the data processing function.

If management decides that it wants to allocate corporate costs among profit centers, the allocation bases chosen should reflect the nature of the indirect costs and their relationship to the profit centers. Thus, costs of centralized corporate services should be allocated on specific bases reflecting the usage factors that cause those costs to be incurred. In this case, cause and benefit may be viewed as practically equivalent criteria. That is, a profit center causes service costs to be incurred to the extent that it perceives it will benefit from those costs. This logic is valid, however, only if a significant portion of the corporate service costs is variable with the volume of usage.

Corporate administrative costs, on the other hand, are caused by the existence and the size of the corporation as a whole, not by activity in individual profit centers. Consequently, the criteria of cause and benefit are unlikely to lead to logical allocation bases. Indeed, since corporate administrative costs are only vaguely related to individual profit centers, it does seem reasonable that they be allocated, if at all, on some very general base, such as a measure of size. And size implies ability to bear. Bigger profit centers can afford to bear larger shares of administrative costs. Such an approach to allocation also seems to meet the highly subjective but widely cited criterion of fairness.

If management is trying to decide whether or not to allocate all corporate indirect costs to profit centers, the ease of selecting a logical allocation base may help in the decision regarding a specific cost item. If a specific allocation base reflects factors that cause the cost to be incurred, the allocation is more likely to be defensible. Conversely, if only a very general base can be found, the allocation may be of little value. Once again, allocations of corporate service costs are more likely to be defensible and useful than are allocations of corporate administrative costs.

Allocations for Performance Evaluation

The theoretical literature on cost allocation almost universally concludes that indirect cost allocations are not economically logical for purposes of performance evaluation. Profit center managers cannot control indirect costs, except by controlling the volume of their demands for corporate services whose costs are largely variable. Otherwise, allocations move costs away from the responsibility centers in which they might be controlled and into others where they cannot be controlled.

Despite this lack of economic logic, however, allocations may be useful for purposes of performance evaluation if they induce desirable patterns of behavior in profit center managers. In other words, there may be behavioral or motivational reasons for making allocations that would otherwise be indefensible. The most widely cited reason for allocating indirect costs for performance evaluation in this study was behavioral—it was to remind profit center managers that indirect costs exist and must be covered by earnings in profit centers.

Many firms also justified allocations for this purpose on the grounds that they would stimulate profit center managers to pressure corporate managers to control their costs. Again, this is a motivational reason that makes economic sense only if it really works. If allocations are to be made principally for behavioral objectives, it follows that the behavior of the profit center managers must be conditioned. The managers must accept the need for the allocations, although not necessarily the amounts allocated.

If allocations are to be used in performance evaluations, costs should be allocated at predetermined rates only. Ideally, variable indirect costs should be allocated at predetermined rates on the basis of actual volume of service or usage, whereas fixed indirect costs should be allocated in a single predetermined lump sum. In practice, however, few companies responding to the survey did allocate fixed and variable costs separately. Moreover, most of them allocated actual costs rather than predetermined amounts to profit centers for purposes of performance evaluation. Thus, the ideal conditions for allocations in this context are usually not present.

At the very least, allocations should be at predetermined amounts if they are to affect compensation paid to profit center managers. In this way, their performances and, hence, their compensation will be affected only by the extent of their use of corporate services and not by the efficiency of corporate staff managers. The behavioral objective of the allocation will be accomplished, and the notion of controlling costs at their sources will be preserved.

Allocations for Cost-Based Pricing

The dominant reasons given for allocating indirect costs for purposes of cost-based pricing were all variations of one fairly obvious theme—the desire to recover a fair share of all costs through the prices of all product lines. Note that this study addressed only one type of pricing policy, that in which price is based upon costs. Prices based simply on competitive market forces are, by definition, not cost-based prices. When the seller does have discretion in pricing its products, it is only logical that they would be based, at least partly, on the seller's costs. Those might be direct costs only, or they might include an allocation of indirect costs. Most of the firms in this survey that did base prices on costs used indirect cost allocations to ensure that all costs, indirect as well as direct, would be recovered. Only a minority relied upon big enough contribution margins to cover indirect costs in the aggregate.

To the extent that indirect costs include variable corporate service costs, their allocation for purposes of pricing is economically logical, as long as the allocation base truly reflects causal factors. To the extent that they include fixed costs of corporate administration, no single allocation method can be defended as better than any other. Thus, the exact amount allocated for purposes of pricing may not be the uniquely correct amount. Nevertheless, *some* allocation is economically plausible, particularly if the purpose is principally to influence profit center managers' pricing practices. In other words, the ultimate purpose of the allocation may be behavioral, as in the case of allocations for performance evaluation.

Allocations for Decision Analysis

For this purpose, behavioral reasons for indirect cost allocations would not be appropriate. Decision analysis of financial variables should be based strictly on economic logic. That statement does not mean that the ultimate decision should not reflect behavioral considerations as well. Indeed, behavioral factors may dominate economic analysis in the final decision, but they should not affect the analysis of financial variables.

In a decision analysis, the only relevant costs are those that will be changed as a result of the decision—the incremental costs. There may well be incremental indirect costs in connection with a particular decision, but the amount of such incremental costs is unlikely to be the same as the amount that would be allocated to cost objectives affected by the decision in accordance with the existing allocation scheme.

In the absence of better information, however, the current allocation rates may be acceptable surrogates for the true but unknown incremental indirect costs. This is more likely to be true for variable service costs than for fixed costs. Fixed costs, if increased at all by a decision, will probably be increased by an amount unrelated to current allocations. Although the use of current allocation rates may alert managers to the likelihood of some indirect cost increase, the decision analysis depends upon a reasonable estimate of the amount of that increase. In any case, the use of present indirect cost allocations as surrogates for true incremental costs should be tested for validity and not merely assumed to be acceptable.

Summary of Recommendations for Practical Applications

Various practical applications of the findings of this survey have been suggested already. These are summarized below in a series of specific recommendations regarding allocations of corporate indirect costs to primary profit centers. These recommendations are based upon both the management accounting literature and the results of this study. Not every firm is likely to adopt every recommendation, of course. Contrary practices may prove effective in some cases. Management should be careful, however, to evaluate the reasons for each practice critically and to review the practice periodically to ensure that it is producing the intended results. Practices that are effective at one time may prove ineffective at a later time because of changed circumstances. The critical appraisal of accounting and control systems is a continuing requirement.

1. The first step in the indirect cost allocation process should be to identify the purposes of the proposed allocations. Consideration should always be given to the alternative of not allocating. That alternative is easier, of course. Thus, there should be an initial presumption against allocation, to be overcome only by some logical argument as to why allocation is more likely to lead to the achievement of management's objectives.

For example, allocation of corporate indirect costs to profit centers for purposes of performance evaluation in those centers is conceptually inappropriate. However, top management may decide that judiciously selected allocations may induce profit center managers to control their usage of corporate services and also induce corporate staff managers to control their costs. The likelihood of such desirable results should be supported logically, and the actual attainment of them should be tested periodically, perhaps by an internal audit staff.

2. If allocations are to be made, indirect costs must be grouped into logical and reasonably homogeneous cost pools. Then a suitable allocation base must be chosen for each pool. To begin with, criteria for selecting an allocation base should be identified clearly. These criteria should be consistent both with the nature of the costs in the pool and with the purpose(s) of the allocation.

For example, if the costs of a corporate data processing center are to be allocated among primary profit centers for the purpose of performance evaluation, the principal criterion for choosing a base should be the causal factors that relate the costs to the data processing services provided to the several profit centers. Only if the costs are allocated along causal lines can the profit center managers do anything about the amounts allocated.

On the other hand, if general corporate administrative costs are to be allocated to profit centers for purposes of cost-based pricing, no causal relationships are likely to be found. Thus, an ability-to-bear criterion is likely to be used in the selection of an allocation base. In any event, the allocation base chosen should meet the selection criteria and should serve the intended purpose of the allocation. If no such base can be identified, the alternative of not allocating at all should be considered again.

3. Indirect cost pools at the corporate level should be identified either as corporate service costs or as corporate administrative costs. Allocations of service costs are more likely to be justifiable, and allocation bases reflecting causal or beneficial relationships are more likely to be found. Greater caution should be exercised in allocating corporate administrative costs. Although they are essential to the existence of the corporation as a whole, no particular relationships to individual profit centers are likely to be found. Hence, any allocation probably will be entirely arbitrary. Such an allocation may still serve some management purpose, but greater care is required to ensure that it does not have some unintended negative consequence.

4. As noted earlier, allocations of indirect costs for purposes of segment performance evaluation are generally considered to be inappropriate. That is, any measure of segment performance that includes allocated shares of indirect costs includes factors that do not really reflect performance in the segment as a separate entity. Hence, indirect cost allocations should not be made if the purpose is to measure true segment performance.

However, if the purpose is to motivate segment managers to adopt some particular pattern of behavior, allocations may prove to be useful. In effect, allocations of indirect costs then become the means by which corporate management communicates target profit figures to profit center managers, with the aim of ensuring that all costs will be recovered. In such a case, the purpose of the allocations should be made clear to segment managers. Moreover, the method of allocation should be consistent with that purpose. Indirect costs should be allocated at predetermined rates, not actual rates. In this way, segment managers will know in advance how much will be allocated to them, either as a total amount or as a rate per unit of some measure of activity that they can control.

If actual allocation rates are used, efficiency or inefficiency in the corporate office or in corporate staffs will be passed along to the segments and included in the measure of their performances. Since segment managers cannot control efficiency at the corporate level, their reactions to the allocations probably will be negative if actual rates are used. The desired motivational effect will not be achieved.

If significant elements of both fixed and variable costs are present in an indirect cost pool, it is generally useful to allocate the two types of costs separately. Fixed costs are best allocated in a single predetermined amount to each segment. Thus, segment managers will know in advance the exact amounts to be allocated to them. The budgeted and actual amounts allocated will be equal and, consequently, will have no effect on the evaluation of segments' performances. Variable costs should be allocated at predetermined rates over the actual volume of service or other activity. Thus, segment managers will know in advance that the "prices" they are charged for corporate services will not change. The total amounts allocated to them will depend upon their usage of those services. Presumably, segments' usage of corporate services is controllable at the segment level and, hence, is properly reflected in their performance measures.

5. It is particularly difficult to provide general guidance for the allocation of indirect costs for purposes of cost-based pricing. By the very meaning of the term, costs are relevant for this purpose. But which costs? Costs directly traceable to individual products are obviously relevant. Indirect costs are relevant to the aggregate pricing policy for all products, but it is not clear what portion of those indirect costs, if any, is relevant to a single product. The notion of a "fair share" is not operationally meaningful. What is "fair" depends on conditions in the markets for the various products, and those conditions may vary from one market to another and from time to time.

If allocations are made to all profit centers in proportion to their sales revenues or payroll, for example, the consequences may be undesirable. Prices set in a particular profit center may prove to be too high or too low for that market, and total corporate profit may be less than the maximum reasonably attainable. Alternatively, even if appropriate prices are established without regard to indirect cost allocations, the consequent profits reported for a segment may not be a valid base for assessing its true profitability or for comparing its profit contribution to those of other segments.

6. The simplest—and invariably most correct—rule for allocating indirect costs for purposes of decision analysis is not to do it! No allocation, *per se,* is relevant to a decision. This does not mean that no amount of indirect costs is relevant. Indeed, the decision analysis should include an estimate of the incremental indirect costs, if any, that will result from implementation of a decision. That incremental amount is not necessarily equal or even close to the amount that would result from an allocation of indirect costs at the rates currently used, however.

A separate allocation rate for variable indirect costs may be a very good basis for estimating incremental variable indirect costs in connection with a decision that involves a modest change in operating volume. It is very unlikely that an allocation rate for fixed costs alone or one that includes both fixed and variable costs will be useful for this purpose. In any case, although the current allocation *may* be a reasonable surrogate for incremental indirect costs, it should not be *assumed* to be so. If allocations are to be used as surrogates for incremental costs, the validity of that practice should be verified by after-the-fact review of a reasonable sample of past decisions. It is quite possible that a review of actual decisions will reveal some other formula for predicting incremental indirect costs. If so, that formula should be used in decision analyses, even if future allocations are still made at the old rate.

Conclusion

This study has revealed that indirect cost allocations are far more widely used than the accounting literature suggests they should be. Obviously, managers find them useful despite their conceptual shortcomings. Moreover, allocation methods used do not seem to reflect concern for some of the more specific cautions found in the literature. Actual costs are allocated more often than predetermined amounts. Allocation bases, however they may be justified, are more often broad measures of activity or size in profit centers than refined measures of causal or beneficial factors. Such arbitrary practices are less objectionable than theory would suggest if the purposes of the allocations are primarily behavioral.

If the allocations are intended simply to stimulate some desired pattern of behavior by profit center managers and if those managers understand and accept the need for the allocations, arbitrary and simplistic allocation methods are probably as good as any others. On the other hand, if the purpose is to measure cost or profit figures that will be regarded as "correct," allocations should be limited to variable costs of corporate services and allocation bases should represent actual causal factors. Such allocations should be useful for purposes of performance evaluation, cost-based pricing, and decision analysis. Allocations of fixed administrative costs, however, should be avoided unless they can be kept completely neutral in their effects on decisions. And, in that case, it is difficult to see how the resultant allocations would be any better than no allocation at all.

Appendix A

Research Methods

A brief discussion of the research methods employed in this study was provided in Chapter 1. For those who are interested, a more detailed description of the various steps in the research program is presented here. The research methods should be of particular interest to those who wish to make a critical evaluation of the findings and conclusions of this study. In addition, in view of the paucity of published empirical studies of cost allocation practices, this appendix may be useful to anyone interested in conducting further research in this area.

The procedures followed in this research project were divided into seven distinct steps. These are listed below in chronological order, although steps 3 and 4 were actually undertaken concurrently.

1. Definition of the objectives and scope of the research
2. Library research
3. Development and field testing of a questionnaire
4. Selection of the sample of firms to be included in the survey
5. Distribution, receipt, coding, and analysis of the questionnaires
6. In-depth interviews with nine selected respondents
7. Evaluation and interpretation of the data and preparation of the research report

Objectives and Scope of the Research

The basic objective of this study was to determine current business practices with respect to the allocations of indirect costs and the reasons for those practices. Potentially, such a study might have delved into a very wide range of business operations. Preliminary discussions with the research director of the National Association of Accountants revealed that separate studies were already in progress in the areas of pricing policies and internal transfer pricing. Thus, this survey limited its concern with pricing to the use of indirect cost allocations in determining cost-based prices to external customers. Furthermore, the study was limited to allocations of corporate indirect costs to primary profit centers. This limitation was necessary in order to make the project manageable and to avoid conflicting evidence on allocations at different levels in corporations. Finally, the study was designed to focus on indirect cost allocations for four purposes: performance evaluation, cost-based pricing, decision analysis, and financial reporting. The first three of these purposes were of principal interest.

Library Research

The conceptual foundation for the survey was an extensive review of the relevant literature. Although this study focuses on actual indirect cost practices, the library research was done first in order to set current practices in a context of widely discussed issues. The questionnaire that followed was then designed to provide empirical evidence on these issues as they are reflected in actual business practice.

Questionnaire Design and Field Testing

The purpose of the questionnaire was to obtain from companies information on the extent of indirect cost allocations, the reasons for choosing to allocate or not allocate indirect costs, how certain indirect costs are allocated, and other related practices. The first version of the questionnaire was reviewed by a division controller of an international corporation and his assistant. The questionnaire was then revised to incorporate their comments and suggestions. The second version was mailed to a small sample of firms for completion and critical comments. A personal interview was then held with each financial executive who answered the questionnaire to discuss its design and any possible improvements.

In the second phase of field testing, potential problems were uncovered with interpretations of the terms "indirect costs" and "divisions." Both related to the variety of practices and terms employed in multilevel organizations. Terms like "division," "group," "product line," and "profit center" have specific meanings in individual companies, especially those with hierarchies of components at various levels of managerial responsibility. Unfortunately, usage of such terms is not uniform among companies. Furthermore, the practical significance of the concept of "indirect costs" was found to differ among the various levels of management responsibility. As a consequence, a decision was made to focus questions in this survey on the allocation of indirect costs incurred by corporate headquarters to the first level of operating segments. Use of the term "primary profit centers" and the selection of fourteen specific indirect cost items were features of the substantially revised questionnaire prepared after the second field test.

The principal reason for choosing the primary level of profit responsibility rather than a lower level for this study was that allocations from corporate headquarters to primary profit centers are generally the same over all such centers. Allocation practices at lower levels of responsibility, on the other hand, may differ from segment to segment within a firm. For example, one controller interviewed in the second phase of field testing stated that no individual in his firm could answer questions about allocation practices at all levels of management and in all segments.

The third version of the questionnaire was field tested once more before it was sent to the research director and to the project advisory committee for their comments and suggestions. The complete questionnaire package, as it was distributed, is reproduced in Appendix B.

Sample Selection

Samples of firms in specific industries and size categories were selected from the 1979 edition of *Standard and Poor's Register of Corporations* according to the following two criteria:

1. Annual sales (net operating revenue in banks and total premiums in insurance companies) were at least $15 million.
2. At least two executives were cited as being responsible for separate operating segments.

The first criterion was chosen somewhat arbitrarily. The second was intended to limit the survey to firms that had more than one primary profit center.

Firms meeting both criteria were then grouped into subsamples according to industries and sizes, as measured by annual revenues. The number selected and the response rate for each industry and size group are reported in the next section. A disproportionate amount of time was spent in selecting a sample of firms in the small size group ($15 million to $100 million in annual revenue) because many firms in that size range do not have multiple profit centers. A more reasonable lower limit on firm size in studies of this type might be $50 million in sales.

Highly diversified corporations are difficult to fit into a single industry group. This study initially selected all 69 corporations listed by *Forbes* as either "multicompanies" or "conglomerates" and grouped them together under the category of "conglomerates." Three of these proved to be subsidiaries of other conglomerates, however, and were excluded from the sample.

Questionnaire Survey

Because of unavoidable delays in the development of the questionnaire, it

TABLE A-1

Questionnaire Response Rates by Industry

Industry	No. of Questionnaires Distributed	No. of Usable Returns	Response Rate
Banking	120	21	17.5
Conglomerates	66	8	12.1
Insurance	60	8	13.3
Retail	90	14	15.6
Service	90	13	14.4
Transportation	60	9	15.0
Manufacturing	280	48	17.1
Unknown	—	2*	—
Total	766	123	16.1**

* Control numbers removed by respondents.

** The difference in response rates among industries is not significant at the 10% level.

was not distributed until late December 1979 and early January 1980—not an ideal time for a survey addressed to accounting executives. Several firms returned the questionnaire unanswered and cited the year-end closing and the complexity of the questionnaire as reasons for not responding.

The overall response rate was 16.1%. Table A-1 shows the numbers of questionnaires distributed and the numbers of usable responses by industries. The difference in response rates among the seven industries was very small statistically. However, when the usable responses are grouped by sizes of the firms, the difference in response rates is highly significant at the 1% level. Table A-2 shows these data.

Firms with annual sales below $100 million were considered small for purposes of this study. Two reasons for the relatively low response rate among these firms were determined by telephone inquiries. First, unlike large firms, small firms usually do not have separate financial planning staffs that deal with cost allocations. Such work is done by accounting department personnel, who were under heavy work pressure during the year-end closing period. Second, many small firms regarded the questionnaire as inapplicable to them; they felt they did not have the type of divisional structure the questionnaire sought to examine.

TABLE A-2

Questionnaire Response Rates by Firm Size

Size of Firms	No. of Questionnaires Distributed	No. of Usable Returns	Response Rate
Small	190	18	9.5
Medium	190	24	12.6
Large	386	79	20.5
Unknown	—	2*	—
Total	766	123	16.1**

* Control numbers removed by respondents.

* * The difference in response rates is significant at the 1% level.

All usable responses were hand-coded for computer processing, with the exception of responses to question 9. This question asked for the allocation bases over which fourteen different indirect cost items were allocated for four separate reasons. The diversity of allocation bases reported here was so great that manual processing of the data was unavoidable.

Five characteristics of the firms were used to examine the answers to each question for possible patterns of differences in allocation practices. These five characteristics are industry, size (as measured by annual revenues), a policy of centralization or decentralization, the number of primary profit centers, and the amount of corporate indirect costs as a percentage of total revenue. Responses according to the first two characteristics were shown in Tables A-1 and A-2, respectively.

The numbers of usable responses classified according to the last three characteristics are reported in Table A-3. The computer printout was checked visually for any potentially significant differences. The selected data were then analyzed statistically. Chi-square tests were used for frequency data and Kendall's rank correlation coefficient of concordance was computed for ranked data. A number of significant differences were found and are reported in the text of this report. Raw data from the questionnaire responses are summarized in Appendix B.

In-Depth Interviews

The last page of the questionnaire asked respondents whether they would

TABLE A-3

Questionnaire Responses Classified by Other Characteristics of Respondents

Demographic Characteristic	Number of Responses
By Responsibility:	
Centralized	50
Decentralized	70
By the Number of Primary Profit Centers:	
1–5	18
6–10	28
11–20	27
21–50	21
51–100	6
Over 100	20
By Total Indirect Cost as a Percentage of Total Sales:	
0–2%	22
2.1%–5%	31
5.1%–10%	16
10.1%–20%	15
Over 20%	26

like to receive a brief summary of the findings and also whether they would be willing to participate in a personal interview with the researchers. A majority of the respondents indicated an interest in the survey results, and about 50% of those were also willing to take part in an interview. In-depth interviews were then conducted at nine firms on the West Coast to explore the rationale behind certain practices and to discuss a few related issues that were not addressed in the questionnaire. These interviews proved to be extremely helpful in interpreting some of the questionnaire responses.

Evaluation of Data and Preparation of the Report

The results of the literature review, the analysis of data collected by the questionnaire, and the results of the personal interviews formed the basis for this final research report.

Appendix B

Survey Questionnaire

The package distributed with the questionnaire included a cover letter signed by the research director of the National Association of Accountants and an introduction that explained the scope of the questionnaire and defined key terms used in it. The complete package is reproduced in the pages that follow. The raw response data compiled from the usable returns are inserted in this copy of the questionnaire, except in the case of question 9, where responses were too numerous and varied to permit any such summary.

National Association of Accountants

919 THIRD AVENUE
NEW YORK, N.Y. 10022
(212) 754-9700

Dear Sir or Madam:

The enclosed questionnaire is being administered in connection with a study of indirect cost allocation conducted by Professors James M. Fremgen and Shu S. Liao of the Naval Postgraduate School on behalf of the National Association of Accountants. I sincerely hope that you will be willing to participate in this study.

The purpose of the questionnaire is to determine the objectives, methods, and extent of indirect cost allocations in business practice. Little direct attention has been given to this universal problem, and there is a real need to document current practices. I am hopeful that this research project will contribute to a better understanding of the effective management of business enterprises.

The questionnaire is being sent to a carefully selected sample of firms with multiple profit or responsibility centers. Your cooperation in responding promptly will aid greatly in the progress of this research. For your convenience, a self-addressed return envelope, requiring no postage, is enclosed.

This questionnaire should be completed by a financial or accounting executive who is familiar with your company's cost allocation practices. All information provided by respondents will be held in strict confidence and will be reported only as part of summarized tabulations, with no identification of individual firms in any way.

I shall be most grateful for your cooperation in this effort to extend our knowledge of management accounting practices.

Very truly yours,

Stephen Landekich
Research Director

Enclosures

National Association of Accountants Questionnaire on Allocation of Indirect Costs

Scope of the Questionnaire

This questionnaire is designed to cover practices currently used in allocating indirect costs among primary profit (responsibility) centers within a firm. The term *INDIRECT COSTS* refers to those costs incurred for the benefit of two or more components of a company in such a way that it is difficult to trace specific portions of those costs exclusively to individual components. The term is synonymous with "common costs." It is used in direct contrast to "direct costs," which are wholly and exclusively traceable to a single component.

Since specific terms used vary from company to company, we use the broadly inclusive term *PRIMARY PROFIT (RESPONSIBILITY) CENTER* to indicate the principal components or segments of a company (e.g., subsidiaries, groups, business units, divisions, departments, branches, or product lines) for which separate financial performances are reported. In companies in which there is a hierarchy of components at various levels of management responsibility, the primary profit (responsibility) centers are those at the highest level of separate responsibility.

The questions that follow address your company's policies with respect to the allocation of indirect costs in general and then with respect to four distinct purposes for which such allocations may or may not be made. These four purposes are as follows:

1. *PERFORMANCE EVALUATION*—This is the periodic measurement and internal reporting of the financial performance of a primary profit center. Typically, actual performance is compared with predetermined performance criteria, such as target profit or return on investment.
2. *COST-BASED PRICING*—This term refers to any policy under which prices of products or services are based either wholly or substantially on the individual company's costs. It is in contrast to the situation in which prices are determined entirely by competitive market forces.
3. *DECISION ANALYSIS*—This term is used to denote analyses made by management of the expected financial consequences of proposed decisions involving choices among alternatives (e.g., introducing new products or services, choosing optimal product mixes, making or buying parts, and replacing equipment).
4. *FINANCIAL REPORTING*—This is the periodic preparation of financial statements in accordance with requirements of the Financial Accounting Standards Board or regulatory agencies for use by external parties.

Thus, several questions will contain four columns or four sets of answers corresponding to these four purposes. A few questions will deal specifically with only one of these purposes, which will be clearly indicated.

1. Do you regard your company essentially as a centralized or as a decentralized organization?

   50 Centralized   70 Decentralized

2. How many primary profit (responsibility) centers report separate operating data (revenues and expenses) in your company?

1 to 5:	18	11 to 20:	27	51 to 100:	6
6 to 10:	28	21 to 50:	21	Over 100:	20

3. Approximately what percentage of your company's total sales (net operating revenue in a bank) was the total of all indirect costs (other than federal income tax) in your most recent fiscal year?

0 to 2%:	22	5 to 10%:	16	Over 20%:	26
0 to 5%:	31	10 to 20%:	15		

4. Does your company allocate any part of these indirect costs among the primary profit (responsibility) centers *for any purpose?*

   103 Yes   20 No

   If you answered "yes" to this question, please complete all of the remaining questions. If you answered "no" to this question, please complete questions 7, 10, 11, and 12 only.

5. The choice of allocation methods may be based upon one or more criteria. Please check as many of the criteria listed below as are applicable to your decisions as to how indirect costs should be allocated.

   75 Benefits received by profit centers from indirect costs.

   81 Factors which cause the indirect costs to be incurred.

   17 A profit center's ability to bear the charge for indirect costs.

   17 A principle that the amount allocated to one profit center should not be affected by actions or conditions in any other profit center.

68 Equity or fairness to all of the parties involved.

13 Other.

6. How often does your company review and, if necessary, make changes to your indirect cost allocation policies and methods?

   67 Annually.

   10 Regularly at intervals longer than one year.

   26 Only when required by major changes in operations or other conditions.

7. Please indicate by checking the appropriate box whether each of the expense categories listed below is (1) all direct costs, (2) all indirect costs, (3) part direct and part indirect, (4) included in one general and administrative expense (G&A) pool, or (5) not applicable at all in your company.

Expense Category	All Direct	All Indirect	Part Direct & Part Indirect	Included in G&A	Not Applicable
G&A expenses	1	38	71		
Research and development	27	16	38	10	
Personnel functions	3	32	60	25	
Accounting	2	26	62	29	
Data processing	9	25	72	14	
Product marketing	46	21	28	17	
Public relations & corporate promotion	1	55	27	33	
Corporate engineering & production	18	18	17	9	
Purchasing	23	33	41	19	
Corporate executives' compensation	4	48	30	37	
Treasurer's functions	3	63	18	34	
Interest on debt	17	52	22	14	
Legal and government affairs	3	49	36	31	
Tax department	1	63	15	37	
Other (please specify)___					

8. This question seeks to determine the extent to which indirect expenses listed in question 7 are allocated to primary profit (responsibility) centers for each of the four purposes identified earlier. Please check the appropriate box *for each purpose* to indicate whether the *full* amount, *part* of the expense, or *none* of it is allocated. (If you answered in question 7 that a particular expense category is included in the G&A pool or is not applicable in your company, simply ignore that expense below.) If pricing policies vary among your primary profit (responsibility) centers, answers in the second column should pertain to those centers in which prices are based substantially on costs.

	Performance Evaluation			Cost-Based Pricing			Decision Analysis			Financial Reporting		
Expense Category	Full	Part	None	Full	Part	None	Full	Part	None	Full	Part	None
G&A expenses	46	27	14	36	17	22	33	18	29	36	26	18
Research & development	35	15	12	23	13	20	26	14	19	29	10	20
Personnel functions	46	20	11	34	9	24	32	13	25	31	20	17
Accounting	44	18	13	31	10	25	28	14	27	32	19	15
Data processing	53	23	10	43	10	22	38	17	21	37	17	19
Product marketing	38	14	9	30	11	17	28	16	15	29	6	20
Public relations & corporate promotion	39	14	19	28	7	27	27	9	28	29	12	24
Corporate engineering & production	25	12	8	20	10	14	20	12	14	21	9	14
Purchasing	46	15	12	38	8	20	33	11	22	34	13	17
Corporate executives' salaries	39	13	19	30	7	25	25	13	28	28	13	23
Treasurer's functions	40	15	17	32	10	22	26	14	26	31	13	21
Interest on debt	39	11	20	29	4	28	29	15	22	31	9	25
Legal and government affairs	41	18	14	30	10	23	26	13	26	31	14	18
Tax department	39	13	16	30	8	24	26	10	27	30	13	18
Other (please specify)____												

9. This question asks about the allocation bases (e.g., total payroll dollars, number of employees, number of hours spent) over which indirect costs are allocated, either in full or in part, for each of the four purposes addressed in this questionnaire. If an item is not allocated for a particular purpose, enter "NA" in that blank. (If you answered in question 7 that a particular expense category is included in the G&A pool or is not applicable to your company, simply ignore that expense below.)

	Allocation Base Used for			
Expense Category	Performance Evaluation	Cost-Based Pricing	Decision Analysis	Financial Reporting
G&A expenses	(For summaries of responses, see Tables 4-2, 4-3, and 4-4.)			____
Research & development	____	____	____	____
Personnel functions	____	____	____	____
Accounting	____	____	____	____
Data processing	____	____	____	____
Product marketing	____	____	____	____
Public relations & corporate promotion	____	____	____	____
Corporate engineering & production	____	____	____	____
Purchasing	____	____	____	____
Corporate executives' salaries	____	____	____	____
Treasurer's functions	____	____	____	____
Interest on debt	____	____	____	____
Legal & government affairs	____	____	____	____
Tax department	____	____	____	____
Other (please specify)	____	____	____	____

Each of the next four questions addresses reasons your company does or does not allocate indirect costs for one of the four purposes referred to in this study. In questions 10, 11, and 12 you will find two columns headed "Reasons for allocating" and "Reasons for Not Allocating." Please use only the first column if you *do* allocate any expense categories, whether in full or in part, for the particular purpose mentioned. Use only the second column if *you do not* allocate any indirect costs at all for that particular purpose.

10. With respect to *performance evaluation,* please indicate the principal reasons for allocating or not allocating indirect costs to primary profit (responsibility) centers. Please choose as many reasons as are applicable and rank them in order of importance by marking the most important reason "1," the second most important "2," etc. (Use only one column.)

Reasons for Allocating

82 To remind profit center managers that indirect expenses exist and that profit center earnings must be adequate to cover some share of those expenses.

52 To relate profit center earnings to total company profit so that the sum of all centers' profits is equal to company profit.

42 To stimulate profit center managers to put pressure on central managers to control service costs.

21 To encourage use of central services that would otherwise be underutilized.

59 Because the allocation methods used fairly reflect each profit center's usage of essential common services.

Reasons for Not Allocating

26 Because indirect costs are not related to individual profit centers and, thus, allocations are arbitrary and tend to distort reported center profits.

5 Because profit center managers cannot agree on a *method* of allocation.

22 Because profit center managers object to charges for expenses that they *cannot control.*

8 Because indirect costs are relatively immaterial in amount and would not significantly affect reported center profits.

9 Because the clerical costs of making the allocations would be greater than any possible benefits.

Reasons for Allocating	Reasons for Not Allocating
7 To minimize state or local taxes.	6 Other.
6 Other.	

11. With respect to *cost-based pricing,* please indicate the principal reasons for allocating or not allocating indirect costs to primary profit (responsibility) centers. Please choose as many reasons as are applicable and rank them in order of importance by marking the most important reason "1," the second most important "2," etc. (Use only one column.)

Reasons for Allocating	Reasons for Not Allocating
56 To recover a fair share of indirect costs in the price of each product line.	20 Because our pricing policy is designed to provide a contribution margin from each product high enough so that all indirect costs are recovered.
50 To remind product line managers that indirect costs exist and must be covered by products' prices, even though prices are not based directly on costs.	28 Because prices are determined by market factors beyond management's control. Cost allocations would not affect them.
19 Because our prices are set by government regulations and the allocation of indirect costs is required by those regulations.	8 Because product line managers are free to set their own prices and their profit margins are adequate to cover indirect costs as well as direct costs.
40 Because the allocation methods used fairly reflect each product's share of essential common costs and, thus, these shares should be included in prices.	18 Because allocations are arbitrary and the resultant "full costs" are not reliable bases for pricing.
2 Other.	5 Other.

12. With respect to *decision analysis*, please indicate the principal reasons for allocating or not allocating indirect costs to primary profit (responsibility) centers. Please choose as many reasons as are applicable and rank them in order of importance by marking the most important reason "1," the second most important "2," etc. (Use only one column.)

Reasons for Allocating

57 Because allocations of indirect costs are relevant to the determination of the effect of a proposed decision on company profit.

28 Because the proposed decision is expected to affect future allocations of indirect costs to profit centers. Thus, the allocation now is intended to inform profit center managers what future allocations are likely to be.

34 Because current indirect cost allocation amounts are considered to be the best available approximations of expected actual increases in indirect cost categories.

5 Other.

Reasons for Not Allocating

37 Because indirect costs, as such, are not expected to be affected by the decisions made and, hence, are irrelevant to the decision analysis.

27 Because the arbitrary nature of allocations tends to create an artificial picture of profits expected to result from decisions.

7 Other.

13. With respect to *financial reporting* for external users, what is your company's position with regard to the allocation of indirect costs to "reportable segments," as required in the FASB's Statement of Financial Accounting Standards No. 14, or similar allocations required by regulatory bodies? (Please check only one answer.)

36 We are not required to report segment profit data and do not do so.

8 We report segment profit data and allocate indirect expenses to segments even though we are not required to do so.

44 We report segment profit data in accordance with requirements and believe that such reporting is appropriate and useful.

13 We report segment profit data and allocate indirect costs only because of requirements but we believe that such data are not useful to investors and other outside users of financial statements.

If you do allocate indirect expenses to segments in reporting segment profit data, what is the principal reason for the extent to which such allocations are made in financial reports? (Please check only one answer.)

35 We believe that our indirect costs allocation practices are exactly in accordance with FASB requirements.

0 We allocate more than the minimum required amount of indirect costs in order to minimize state or local taxes.

14 We allocate more than the minimum required amount of indirect costs because we believe that the resulting profit data provide a better picture of our company's profitability.

5 Other.

14. Does your company allocate variable indirect costs and fixed indirect costs separately for each of the following purposes?

	Yes	No
Performance evaluation	28	68
Cost-based pricing	25	65
Decision analysis	25	69
Financial reporting	22	70

15. For each of the four purposes listed below, please indicate whether the amounts of indirect costs allocated to primary profit (responsibility) centers are actual or predetermined amounts. If they are predetermined, please indicate whether variances from actual

amounts are also allocated in the same proportions or are left unallocated.

	Actual	Pre-determined	If predetermined, variances are Allocated	Unallocated
Performance evaluation	41	40	9	31
Cost-based pricing	33	29	5	24
Decision analysis	36	31	6	25
Financial reporting	39	26	9	17

Thank you very much for your help in this research project.

If you wish to receive a brief summary of the results of this study, please indicate the name and address of the person to whom it should be sent.

____

____

____

As part of the research, a limited number of personal interviews with questionnaire respondents will be scheduled. This interview would take less than an hour, and no comments would be attributed to either individuals or companies. If you would be willing to participate in such an interview, please indicate the name and address of the person to be contacted (if different from the one given above).

We would be willing to participate in a personal interview.

Yes 44 No 79

Name and address of person to be contacted.

____

____

____

Bibliography

American Institute of Certified Public Accountants, *Accounting Research and Terminology Bulletins: Final Edition* (New York: American Institute of Certified Public Accountants, 1971).

Anthony, Robert N., and Glenn A. Welsch, *Fundamentals of Management Accounting*, revised edition (Homewood, Ill.: Richard D. Irwin, Inc., 1977).

Backer, Morton, and Walter B. McFarland, *External Reporting for Segments of a Business* (New York: National Association of Accountants, 1968).

Baumes, Carl G., *Allocating Corporate Expenses*, Business Policy Study No. 108 (New York: National Industrial Conference Board, Inc., 1963).

Beckett, John A., "A Study of the Principles of Allocating Costs," *The Accounting Review*, XXVI (July 1951).

Bodnar, George, and Edward J. Lusk, "Motivational Considerations in Cost Allocation Systems: A Conditioning Theory Approach," *The Accounting Review*, LII (October 1977).

Boeing Company, *Towards Common Concepts of Cost Allocations in Cost Accounting* (Seattle: The Boeing Company, 1978).

Brummet, R. Lee, *Overhead Costing* (Ann Arbor: University of Michigan, 1957).

Comptroller General of the United States, *Report on the Feasibility of Applying Uniform Cost Accounting Standards to Negotiated Defense Contracts* (Washington, D.C.: Government Printing Office, 1970).

Cost Accounting Standards Board, *Restatement of Objectives, Policies, and Concepts* (Washington, D.C.: Cost Accounting Standards Board, 1977).

Department of Defense, *Defense Acquisition Regulations*.

Financial Accounting Standards Board, *Financial Reporting for Segments of a Business Enterprise*, Statement of Financial Accounting Standards No. 14 (Stamford, Conn.: Financial Accounting Standards Board, 1976).

——, *Qualitative Characteristics of Accounting Information*, Statement of Financial Accounting Concepts No. 2 (Stamford, Conn.: Financial Accounting Standards Board, 1980).

Fremgen, James M., *Accounting for Managerial Analysis*, 3rd edition (Homewood, Ill.: Richard D. Irwin, Inc., 1976).

Horngren, Charles T., *Cost Accounting: A Managerial Emphasis*, 4th edition (Englewood Cliffs, N.J.: Prentice-Hall, Inc., 1977).

Jensen, Daniel L., "A Class of Mutually Satisfactory Allocations," *The Accounting Review*, LII (October 1977).

Joyce, James E., "The Overhead Mystique," *Management Accounting*, L (November 1968).

Kendall, M.G., *Rank Correlation Methods*, 2nd edition (London: Charles Griffin & Company, Ltd., 1955).

Landekich, Stephen, "Cost Allocations to Inventory," *Management Accounting*, LIV (March 1973).

McGuigan, James R., and R. Charles Moyer, *Managerial Economics* (Hinsdale, Ill.: The Dryden Press, 1975).

Mautz, Robert K., *Financial Reporting by Diversified Companies* (New York: Financial Executives Research Foundation, 1968).

Moriarity, Shane, "Another Approach to Allocating Joint Costs," *The Accounting Review*, L (October 1975).

National Association of Accountants, *Accounting for Costs of Capacity*, Research Report No. 39 (New York: National Association of Accountants, 1963).

______, *Costing Joint Products*, Research Series No. 31 (New York: National Association of Accountants, 1957).

National Association of Cost Accountants, "Product Costs for Pricing Purposes," *NACA Bulletin*, XXXIV (August 1953).

Neuner, John J. W., and Edward B. Deakin, III, *Cost Accounting: Principles and Practice*, 9th edition (Homewood, Ill.: Richard D. Irwin, Inc., 1977).

Rappaport, Alfred, and Eugene M. Lerner, *Segment Reporting for Managers and Investors* (New York: National Association of Accountants, 1972).

Reece, James S., and William R. Cool, "Measuring Investment Center Performance," *Harvard Business Review* (May–June 1978).

Shillinglaw, Gordon, *Managerial Cost Accounting*, 4th edition (Homewood, Ill.: Richard D. Irwin, Inc., 1977).

Skousen, K. Fred, "A Format for Reporting Segment Profits," *Management Accounting*, LII (June 1971).

Solomons, David, *Divisional Performance: Measurement and Control* (Homewood, Ill.: Richard D. Irwin, Inc., 1965).

Staubus, George J., *Activity Costing and Input–Output Accounting* (Homewood, Ill.: Richard D. Irwin, Inc., 1971).

Thomas, Arthur L., *The Allocation Problem in Financial Accounting Theory,* Studies in Accounting Research No. 3 (Evanston, Ill.: American Accounting Association, 1969).

______, *The Allocation Problem:* Part Two, Studies in Accounting Research No. 9 (Sarasota, Fla.: American Accounting Association, 1974).

______, *A Behavioral Analysis of Joint Cost Allocation and Transfer Pricing* (Champaign, Ill.: Stipes Publishing Company, 1980).

______, "The FASB and the Allocation Fallacy," *Journal of Accountancy* (November 1975).

______, "Useful Arbitrary Allocations," *The Accounting Review,* XLVI (July 1971).

Vancil, Richard F., *Decentralization: Managerial Ambiguity by Design* (Homewood, Ill.: Dow Jones–Irwin, 1978).

Weber, Charles, *The Evolution of Direct Costing* (Urbana: University of Illinois, 1966).

Wright, Howard W., and James P. Bedingfield, "Benefit as a Criterion for Indirect Cost Allocation," *The Federal Accountant,* XXII (September 1973).

Zimmerman, Jerold L., "The Costs and Benefits of Cost Allocations," *The Accounting Review,* LIV (July 1979).

National Association of Accountants Committee on Research 1980–81

Calvin A. Vobroucek
Chairman
Caterpillar Tractor Company
Peoria, Illinois

George Bannon
Bethlehem Steel Corporation
Bethlehem, Pennsylvania

Richard F. Bebee
Alexander Grant & Company
Chicago, Illinois

Robert U. Boehman
Jasper Rubber Products
Jasper, Indiana

Germain Boer
Vanderbilt University
Nashville, Tennessee

Paul E. Dascher
Drexel University
Philadelphia, Pennsylvania

Dwight H. Davis
A. O. Smith Corporation
Kankakee, Illinois

Paul H. Davis
International Harvester Company
San Diego, California

Geraldine F. Dominiak
Texas Christian University
Fort Worth, Texas

Patricia P. Douglas
University of Montana
Missoula, Montana

J. Bernard Eck
May Zima & Company
Daytona Beach, Florida

Michael L. Ferrante
Ernst & Whinney
White Plains, New York

Penny A. Flugger
Morgan Guaranty Trust Company
New York, New York

Theodore C. Gearhart
GAO-IRS
Washington, D.C.

Charles L. Grant
Becton Dickinson & Company
Rochelle Park, New Jersey

John L. Hanson
Electro Corporation
Sarasota, Florida

John H. Holzapfel
Coopers & Lybrand
Pittsburgh, Pennsylvania

Henry M. Klein
General Instrument
El Paso, Texas

Ira Landis
Laventhol & Horwath
Los Angeles, California

Paul H. Levine
Magnetic Analysis Corporation
Mt. Vernon, New York

Jack E. Meadows
Combustion Engineering Company
Chattanooga, Tennessee

Thomas J. O'Reilly
Coopers & Lybrand
Cleveland, Ohio

Ronald J. Patten
University of Connecticut
Storrs, Connecticut

Howard O. Rockness
Dartmouth College
Hanover, New Hampshire

W. Peter Salzarulo
Miami University
Oxford, Ohio

Bruce T. Santilli
Abex Corporation
Winchester, Virginia

Fred S. Schulte
Tracor, Inc.
Austin, Texas

Henry A. Schwartz
IBM
Armonk, New York

Milton F. Usry
Oklahoma State University
Stillwater, Oklahoma